SPECIAL COLLECTOR'S EDITION

Sports Illustrated PRESENTS

THE CHICAGO BULLS

THREE SEASONS TO SAVOR

33

BILL SMITH

Sports Illustrated

COVER PHOTOGRAPH BY
ANDREW D. BERNSTEIN/NBA PHOTOS

Ring! Ring! Ring!

As this banner outside the team's front offices made abundantly clear, the Chicago Bulls answered the call once again.

Before Jordan

The Bulls played without His Airness for 18 years. Most of that time they were pretty good; the rest of that time they were very bad

Until Jordan arrived, Sloan was Mr. Bull.

LANE STEWART

Klein said, "I imagine we will be

Under Motta, Love (a.k.a. Butterbean) . . .

BY HANK HERSCH

Before the Chicago Bulls were born, in 1966, there were the Chicago American Gears, the Chicago Bruins and the Chicago Studebakers of the then long-defunct National Basketball League, as well as the Chicago Stags, the Chicago Packers and the Chicago Zephyrs of the NBA. Before the Bulls had Michael Jordan, they had Big Red and the Blond Bomber; Flingin' Flynn and the Gem; the Jet, Spider, Big Daddy, Butterbean and Stormin' Norman; the Big A, Dr. K and Dr. Junk. And before Jordan and the Bulls brought championship hoop to the Loop, it was accepted as gospel that pro basketball would never fly in Chi.

Imagine that. Imagine today's decibel level at Chicago Stadium and the worldwide demand for Bullabilia. Then imagine that not too long ago, in the city of the big shoulders and the low-post mentality, locals would have just as soon taken a January jump in Lake Michigan as a seat at an NBA game. But that was the way it was in the Second City. "Long regarded as the burial grounds of professional basketball," wrote *The Sporting News* in 1966, Chicago was a town already sated by the Bears, the Blackhawks, the Cubs and the White Sox. To take a measure of the game's futility in Chicago just consider the metamorphosis of the Packers, who after their first season, 1961–62, felt compelled to change their name to the Zephyrs, a name made fitting when they wafted away to Baltimore the following year.

Undaunted by this state of affairs, a 6′ 8″ businessman, former Northwestern basketball player and ex–American Gear named Dick Klein led a group of five investors who shelled out a total of $1.6 million to the nine-team NBA for an expansion franchise in February 1966. The night before the new Chicago club's initial press conference, Klein came up with its nickname. "All I could think of was Bulls," he said. "I imagine we'll be called the Ferdinands when we lose."

The Bulls set up shop at the 11,002-seat International Amphitheatre, located among the stockyards and slaughterhouses on the South Side. Then they set about attracting attention. Every day cigar-chomping publicist Ben Bentley did his shoe-leather shtick, making a personal pitch to each of the four local papers. "There's nothing like meeting eyeball to eyeball with a writer and throwing him an angle he can use," Bentley says. The promotions director, 26-year-old Jerry Colangelo, rented a flatbed truck and wheeled a snorting bull down Michigan Avenue. "Our total season-ticket sale that first year was less than one hundred," says Colangelo, now president of the Phoenix Suns. "I think that stunt got us about two more orders."

The expansion draft in the spring yielded 18 players, the two most significant ones coming from those erstwhile Packers/Zephyrs, the Baltimore Bullets: guard Jerry Sloan, who had just completed his rookie season, and veteran center Johnny (Big Red) Kerr, who at 33 gave up his playing career to become the Bulls' coach. Kerr, a Chicago native who had been a star at Illinois, was colorful and quotable. He rode the refs, pounded the floor with a knotted white towel and prescribed LSD for his players—not the stuff Timothy Leary was then extolling but a

. . . and Walker became the top forward pairing.

called the Ferdinands when we lose."

In 1981–82, the Luvabulls had little to cheer about.

"loose, scrambling defense." In the Bulls' first trade, Klein acquired San Francisco Warrior playmaker Guy Rodgers, who wound up setting the NBA single-season assist mark while running Kerr's freewheeling, "fast weave" offense in 1966–67. Kerr earned Coach of the Year honors by winning 33 games, which is still the NBA record for an expansion franchise, and taking Chicago to the playoffs.

Less promising than the won-loss record was the average home attendance of 4,772 fans, an especially feeble number given that the Bulls spared no hype. Taking a page from the marketing of football star Paul (Golden Boy) Hornung, Chicago promoted its top pick, Dave Schellhase from Purdue, as the Blond Bomber. The Bomber turned out to be a dud. Kerr also oversold his injured big man, Nate Bowman, a career 2.9 points-a-game scorer, mentioning him in the same breath as Bill Russell. (A more realistic Bentley said of Bowman, "Nate the Great, you're trading bait.") And Bowman wasn't Kerr's only post problem: center Len Chappell, it turned out, couldn't catch bounce passes because he wore contact lenses. But then, the whole history of the Chicago Bulls B.J. (Before Jordan) should not so much be written as recorded on an old 45 with a hole in the middle, so constant was their search for a center. (A search, some would say, that spins on.)

Because of a fire at McCormick Place, Chicago's convention center, the Bulls were ousted from the cozy Amphitheatre by the relocated convention business and had to move uptown to the stadium for their second season. In the city where a lantern-kicking cow lives on in infamy, fires have a particularly notori-

LOVE AND WALKER: HEINZ KLUETMEIER (2); CHEERLEADERS: TONY TRIOLO

"This guy's as crazy as Sloan," Motta said

Stormin' was an apt nickname for Norman.

of Van Lier. "That's my kind of man."

ous place in history, and this one would too: It was a bad omen. Klein, hoping to build through the draft, traded the 32-year-old Rodgers to the Cincinnati Royals for two picks and guard Flingin' Flynn Robinson. (Remember that name.)

Chicago got off to a 1–15 start in 1967–68 and missed the playoffs, with a 29–53 record. Kerr's slogan for his undersized team, "Fight, fire and fall back," sounded more like the tack he took with management; he quit at the end of the season to coach the first-year Suns. Attendance dropped to 3,975 a game, which made sitting in the 17,222-seat stadium as lonely as taking a midnight ride on the El.

The Bulls' one bright spot was the 6′ 5″ Sloan, who, as a rookie out of Evansville, had been buried on the Baltimore bench. He played 48 minutes against the St. Louis Hawks in Chicago's first game and would remain a stalwart over the next 10 seasons, averaging 35.6 minutes, 14.7 points and 7.7 rebounds a game. Good numbers—but Sloan's game could not be reduced to numbers. As the best perimeter defender in the league, he was called either Spider or the Human Chain Saw for the way he hacked away at his opponent's anatomy and will. Thickly built and earthbound, he seemed more a hoops version of Dick Butkus than a precursor of Michael Jordan. And yet in his chin-out aggression and unshakable nerve, it is Air who is Sloan's heir.

Still, Sloan and Co. put themselves in a bind that would plague Chicago for years to come: They were good enough to prevent the Bulls from drafting first but not good enough to finish high in the standings. This quandry did little to fill seats at the Stadium. After a home game in November 1968, Chicago announced a crowd of 891, prompting NBA commissioner Walter Kennedy to reprimand Klein for reporting a figure without a comma in it. Soon thereafter Bentley gave out gate totals of 1,005 and 1,006 and, appropriately enough in the Mayor Daley era, issued a recount for that November game, at which the turnout had somehow swelled to 1,384. Still, the home crowds dropped for the second straight season, to an official count of 3,795 a game. The Bulls seemed poised to go the way of the Studebakers as Klein anticipated a third straight year of six-digit losses.

But beyond the debit sheet, things were looking up. In 1968 Klein drafted 7-foot, 265-pound Tom (Big Daddy) Boerwinkle, who would become a devastating pick-setter and high-post passer in Chicago for the next decade. Klein acquired two more stalwarts from Milwaukee, guard Bob Weiss and forward Bob (Butterbean) Love, for Flingin' Flynn. And to replace Kerr, Klein hired 36-year-old Dick Motta from Weber State—or as he was known in Chicago, "Dick *who*? From Weber *where*?" While Motta had made a modest name for himself in the college ranks, he had seen only a couple of pro games. In announcing Motta's hiring Klein said, "Dick's college teams were well drilled, they knew what they were do-

VAN LIER: WALTER IOOSS JR.; MAY, GILMORE AND VAN LIER: LANE STEWART

Before Air, the Bulls had hair, just cheok out (from left) Scott May, Gilmore and Van Lier.

"If you listen to the fans," Kerr told

Thurmond was no longer Nate the Great by the time he got to Chicago.

Thorn, "you wind up sitting with them."

ing, worked hard and played rough."

Motta played rough too. He took on everything and everyone—including his boss. While Klein had shown an eye for talent, he had made his share of mistakes, like when he drafted Clem (the Gem) Haskins instead of Walt Frazier in 1967 and when, a year later, he traded Keith Erickson for the Los Angeles Lakers' Erwin Mueller when he could have had Baltimore's Gus Johnson. Motta viewed some of Klein's other moves as even more debilitating, designed strictly to cut costs. "I felt like throwing a dollar on the floor to see if it could play for us," Motta snapped after one loss.

If the early Bulls had a watershed season, it was 1969–70. In a move designed to shore up his front office and spark excitement, Klein hired 28-year-old Pat Williams as executive vice-president, luring him away from the Philadelphia 76ers, who had just set a team attendance record. Williams, a devotee of White Sox owner and huckster Bill Veeck, vowed to attract crowds with "anything clean, legal and moral." He quickly skirted the boundaries of all three. For a halftime wrestling exhibition he hired Victor the Bear despite an Illinois law that made "watching the fighting or baiting of a bear" a $200 fine. The Anti-Cruelty Society finally approved the promotion as long as Victor's opponent was known beforehand. Williams was pinned in one fall.

Williams did not come to Chicago alone. At the time Klein was dickering with Philly for Williams's services, the 76ers were trying to pry forward Jimmy Washington, who had been a star at Villanova in Philadelphia, away from the Bulls. Both clubs got their wishes: After one press conference to herald the hiring of Williams, the Bulls held another to announce the acquisition of 6′ 6½″ forward Chet (the Jet) Walker from the Sixers.

A prolific scorer with a deft fallaway jump shot, the 29-year-old Walker was thought to be nearing the end of his prime. The 6′ 8″ Love, Chicago's other forward, was not thought to be capable of one. In three NBA seasons he had never averaged more than seven points a game, and the Bulls nearly shipped him to the Seattle SuperSonics in the summer of 1969. Walker was silky smooth, a linchpin on the 1966–67 Philadelphia club then considered the best in NBA history; Love was gangly and shy, self-conscious because of a stutter. But under Motta, who designed an intricate, picking offense that routinely got his forwards the ball close to the basket, Walker and Love attained a gorgeous synergy: Walker using his rump to gain position and then shooting over his defender with deceptive quickness; Love in constant motion, back-cutting for easy buckets or pump-faking once, twice, three times before firing in a line-drive jumper. In 1969–70 they each poured in more than 20 points a game and for the next five seasons held sway as the most productive forward tandem in the league.

The Bulls of the '70s didn't suit Badger's style.

"I remember I saw Bean get 49 points in back-to-back games [in 1973] shooting that little fallaway jumper of his, and it seemed like every shot went about an eighth of an inch over some bigger guy's hand," Boerwinkle recalls. "The best line I ever heard about Bob was that he could get into a phone booth with Wilt Chamberlain and still get his shot off." And Walker? "He was one of the best clutch players of all time," Boerwinkle says. "There were some tight games in which in the last two minutes we would literally go to Chet every time down the floor. The huddles in timeouts wouldn't be so much to set up plays as to say, 'O.K., Chet, where do you want the ball?' "

Home attendance shot up to 10,050 a game in 1969–70, and the next season the Bulls went 51–31 for their first winning record. Meanwhile, between his battles with Motta and the high rent that Arthur Wirtz, owner of Chicago Stadium, was extracting for the use of his building, Klein was losing his grip on the club. In '72 his group sold out to Wirtz for $5.1 million.

With Klein out of power, Williams satisfied Motta's craving for a playmaker in 1971 by swiping Norm Van Lier from Cincinnati. Stormin' Norman was a perfect fit on the Bulls: a gifted ball handler, tenacious ball hawk and as combative as Sloan. The season before, in fact, the two had duked it out both during a game and in a hallway afterward, prompting Motta to remark, "This guy's as crazy as Sloan. That's my kind of man." Once paired in the backcourt, Sloan and Van Lier took more charges than Marshall Fields. "Those guys woke up every morning making two lists," Williams says. "The first was what they were going to do. The second was who they were going to do it to."

Indeed, in tracing the family tree of the Bad Boy Detroit Pistons of the 1980s, one would find its roots in the Motta Bulls, who played defense with a feral hunger. In 1974 columnist Leonard Lewin issued a warning to the league in *The New York Post*: "Anyone playing the Bulls is advised to get a tetanus shot."

But Chicago had one intractable problem in the early 1970s: geography. As good as the Bulls were, they were in a Western Conference that also had

THURMOND: NEIL LEIFER; BADGER: JOHN IACONO

Gilmore was 7'2" and 240 pounds of

Centers like Dave Corzine had fans begging for . . .

the Milwaukee Bucks of Lew Alcindor/Kareem Abdul-Jabbar and Oscar Robertson (obtained from Cincinnati for—you got it—Flingin' Flynn) and the Los Angeles Lakers of Chamberlain and Jerry West. The Bulls made the playoffs five of their first six seasons but never advanced past the first round. Finally, in '74, they beat Detroit in a seven-game series, but Sloan injured his foot early in Game 6—though he still played for three quarters. Without the Human Chain Saw, the Bulls were buzzed by the Bucks in Round 2.

In the off-season, Motta, now acting as general manager with Williams having departed to the Atlanta Hawks the year before, traded 6′ 9″ backup center Clifford Ray to the Golden State Warriors for 33-year-old center Nate Thurmond, a six-time All-Star. "You have to have the cards to win in this league," Motta said, "and now we've got them." After having given a tryout to Zvonimir Petricevic, a 7-foot Yugoslav, in the 1960s and fallen just short of acquiring Chamberlain in the '70s, Chicago had finally landed its center. But Thurmond turned out to be less Nate the Great than Trading Bait: He averaged fewer than eight points a game.

Without Williams as a buffer between the volatile Motta and his players, the Bulls bickered nonstop, but they fed off the hostility. They won the Midwest, willed themselves to the conference finals, took a three-games-to-two lead over the Warriors—and collapsed. They botched Game 6 at home and blew a 14-point lead in Game 7 as Ray helped the Warriors to a series victory and eventually to the NBA title. Motta lost his last ounce of locker-room respect when, according to the players, he suggested that they vote only partial playoff shares to Van Lier and Love because the two had held out in contract squabbles early in the season. (Motta denied making this suggestion.) Chicago won only 24 games in 1975–76, while Motta variously called his team "a cesspool" and a "circus of sickness." He was gone after the season.

A year later, only Boerwinkle and Van Lier remained from the nucleus of a stout-hearted club that had earned the respect of a city that had shoveled dirt on

CORZINE: PAUL BERESWILL; GILMORE: TONY TOMSIC

immovable muscle and immense Afro.

. . . a stalwart defender in the post like Gilmore.

five previous pro franchises. So as fate would cruelly have it, the party broke up just when the present everyone had wished for finally arrived. Artis (the Big A) Gilmore, picked up from the Kentucky Colonels in the 1976 ABA dispersal draft, was 7′ 2″ and 240 pounds of immovable muscle and immense Afro. And while he may not have dominated—it seemed at times that the gentle Gilmore preferred golf and scuba diving to hoops—he gave Chicago six respectable seasons at center and lent stability to the B.J. Bulls, who certainly needed it.

A parade of seven coaches came and went between 1976–77 and '84–85. Before his first season, Ed Badger, who replaced Motta, requested WIN 50 plates for his car, but some more realistic civil service employee in the state licensing office sent him ones that read WIN 20. Badger did, winning 44, including 20 of his last 24 games. When Badger resigned after the next season, his successor, Larry Costello, lasted 56 games, or as long as it took him to figure out that guard Wilbur (Dr. Junk) Holland was deaf in his left ear and not just ignoring him. After Costello, in rapid-fire fashion, came Scotty Robertson, Sloan, Rod Thorn, Paul Westhead and Kevin Loughery, who ushered in the Jordan era.

That era almost didn't happen. The Costello and Robertson coaching tag team of 1978–79 went 31–51 and Chicago finished last in the Western Conference, earning a coin flip for the top draft choice with the Lakers, who owned the Utah Jazz's choice. At stake: the rights to Magic Johnson. The Bulls held a fan vote to decide which way to call the flip. The public picked heads, and even though Thorn, then the team's general manager, had a strong hunch that Chicago should go with tails, he felt he couldn't go against the fans' choice. When the Bulls' staff gathered on the 13th floor at 333 North Michigan—a floor no other tenant wanted, so Wirtz, the owner of the building, assigned it to the team—for a phone hookup and informed the Lakers of their fan poll results, L.A. graciously let the Bulls call the toss.

There was a pause as commissioner Larry O'Brien flipped the coin and announced the verdict: tails. A celebration of Laker fans roared over the speakerphone. Kerr, back in Chicago as a Bulls' broadcaster, gave Thorn some overdue words of advice. "If you listen to the fans," he said, "sooner or later you wind up sitting with them." Having lost a flip for Alcindor when he was with the Suns, Kerr also told Thorn of the approach he had used to deal with disappointed Phoenicians: "I told them I wanted Neal Walk [a decidedly less promising center] anyway." Of course, who would have believed Thorn if he had said he wanted David Greenwood, Chicago's choice in the 1979 draft, anyway?

The Bulls had to use more than their share of spin control in those days. Greenwood, a 6′ 9½″ All-America from UCLA, would be a solid pro, but he was no Magic. Delmer Beshore, a guard out of Cal, was a terrific name, but he was no NBA point guard (except in Chicago in 1979–80). Larry (Dr. K) Kenon was a fair small forward, but he was no Bernard King, whom Chicago passed on to sign Dr. K in '80. Reggie Theus was an All-Star scorer and looker, but he was no franchise player. Loughery was a fine coach, but he was no model of patience: He wanted to file an official protest of a December '83 game at Houston before the game ended. Erroneously informed by a substitute ref that he had to produce $500 on the spot to lodge the complaint, Loughery fumbled around for some dough, finally produced a piece of plastic and asked, "Will you take American Express?"

No, but the next year the Bulls would take Jordan in the draft, and 18 years of paying their dues would finally pay off. ■

ANDY HAYT

Sloan was the NBA's best defensive guard.

VISITORS
HOME
CHICAGO STADIUM
HOME OF THE BULLS
NEXT HOME GAME

MADE IN THE SHADE

Nine years ago a flip of a coin, poor judgment by the Trail Blazers and a rotten finish by the Bulls combined to provide a sunny future for Chicago and a kid from Carolina

BY MARK VANCIL

Eighteen times a rare silver dollar had been flipped into the air, and 18 times the coin had flattened out with all eyes transfixed on its top side. On May 23, 1984, executives from the Houston Rockets and the Portland Trail Blazers gathered at the league's headquarters, in New York City, for the final rendition of this NBA ritual before the introduction of the lottery the next year. No one who was on hand that day had any idea that the last landing of the 100-year-old coin would produce a revolution in Chicago. ● Houston, despite the presence of 7′ 4″ rookie Ralph Sampson, had limped into this game of chance by taking no chances of its own. The Rockets had closed the season with five straight defeats to edge the San Diego (now Los Angeles) Clippers for last place in the Western Conference. Portland had arrived thanks to a 1981 trade with the Indiana Pacers that sent center Tom Owens to the Pacers for their first-round draft choice in 1984. To Portland's delight, Indiana had held off a hard charge by the Chicago Bulls, who finished 1–14, to guarantee that the Pacers wound up last in the Eastern Conference. ● The coin came to rest. Portland owner Larry Weinberg had called tails. It came up heads, giving Houston the right to select Hakeem Olajuwon, the 7-foot center from the University of Houston and the player everyone most coveted. Back home in Wilmington, N.C., Michael Jordan, who was a junior at North Carolina, sighed.

BOB DONNAN

LANE STEWART

It was music to Jordan's ears when he learned that he would be a Top 5 draft pick as a junior.

The process that had enticed Jordan to leave North Carolina a year short of graduation had begun in Philadelphia. Billy Cunningham, a former Tar Heel who was the 76er coach, had been summoned to Chapel Hill by North Carolina coach Dean Smith. Smith wanted to know how high Jordan would be picked if he opted for the draft. Smith had followed the league standings, and as winter turned toward spring, he had begun calling NBA executives whose teams were positioned to have one of the top five picks. One of those teams happened to be the 76ers, who owned the first pick of the Clippers, one of the league's worst teams.

Though others had helped Smith paint the picture of Jordan's pro future, none provided more color than Cunningham. His Sixers had won the NBA title in 1983, and though they would win 52 games in 1983–84, their brightest star, Julius Erving, was clearly on the back side of a brilliant career. In Jordan, Cunningham saw the future. He assured Smith that if the standings remained the same—the Sixers were looking at the No. 3 pick at the time—they would select Jordan if he was still available. For Smith and Jordan the discussion largely ended there.

But the jockeying for position was far from over. The Bulls' woeful finish enabled them to jump to the third spot in the draft, with a 27–55 record. What's more, the Clippers wound up 30–52, dropping the 76ers' pick to fifth. Philadelphia tried to make a deal with the Bulls, but Chicago wasn't interested. "[Bull general manager] Rod Thorn wanted me," says Jordan. "Somebody else in the organization wanted a big man. But I knew Rod wanted me at that spot."

Chicago had gotten itself into a public-relations mess earlier in the season by trading All-Star guard Reggie Theus, the franchise's most popular player. That trade left the Bulls with lackluster guards Ronnie Lester, Quintin Dailey, Ennis Whatley and Mitchell Wiggins, along with the legendary tandem of Wallace Bryant and Jawann Oldham at center. In other words, they needed help at every position.

"The only obvious thing about the draft was that Olajuwon would be picked by whatever team won the coin flip," says Thorn, now the league's vice-president of operations. "With Portland, I think once their doctor cleared [Kentucky All-American center] Sam Bowie [who had suffered several leg injuries], they didn't have any interest in Jordan because they already had [guards] Clyde Drexler and Jim Paxson. But we were going to take Jordan Number 2 or Number 3. If I had had the first pick, though, I would've taken Olajuwon. Anyone other than Olajuwon, though, you had to use it on Jordan."

RICHARD MACKSON

Olajuwon was everyone's No. 1 pick.

Nonetheless, the Bulls talked to the Trail Blazers about obtaining the No. 2 pick. Some members of the Chicago organization felt that the team should draft Bowie. Jonathan Kovler, the Bulls' managing partner at the time, remembers listening to coach Kevin Loughery, as well as assistants Bill Blair and Fred Carter, plead for a big man.

Portland suffered alone with Bowie.

CARL SKALAK

Kovler also recalls fielding calls from Philadelphia, where 76er owner Harold Katz had caught Cunningham's enthusiasm for Jordan. "They were very high on Jordan, but the center spot was our biggest weakness," says Kovler. "We had discussions about Bowie, [Kentucky center] Mel Turpin and [Auburn forward] Charles Barkley. We also talked to Houston about Hakeem, but nothing ever worked out. The bottom line is that, no matter what we almost did or didn't do, we drafted and signed Michael Jordan."

Get this, though: Virtually everything that has happened to the Bulls since June 19, 1984, the date of that year's collegiate draft, could just as easily have happened to the Rockets. After Philadelphia dropped into the No. 5 position and before the coin flip, Jordan set his sights on the Rockets—particularly Sampson.

Ever since high school Jordan had wondered what it would be like to play on the same team with Sampson. "I wanted to go to Virginia because I wanted to play with Ralph for his last two years of college," says Jordan. "He would have been going into his junior year when I started college. So I wrote Virginia, but they just sent me an admission form. No one came and watched me, nothing like that. Then I visited North Carolina. I was happy with the atmosphere, so I committed early."

Four years later the Rockets committed early too. Their coach, Bill Fitch, was more intrigued with the notion of starting Olajuwon alongside Sampson than he was with pairing Sampson and Jordan. Still, if the Rockets had lost that coin flip, Houston would have been home to another space program. Besides the thought of joining Sampson, Jordan liked the idea of playing in a city with a more Carolina-like climate than most other NBA cities'.

"It all relied on the flip of a coin," says Jordan. "If Portland had won the flip, I knew I was going to the Rockets with the second pick. I knew that. They had Ralph, and they didn't really have a two guard. Like I said, I had wanted to go to Virginia, and they never came after me. So I was looking forward to going to the Rockets."

Jordan pauses for a moment and then says, "Funny how things turn out.".

Yes and no. Yes, if you're the Bulls, not exactly if you're the Trail Blazers. Portland had been involved in three coin flips before unlucky number 19. The only time the Trail Blazers won the toss, in 1972, they drafted LaRue Martin with the No. 1 pick. The Buffalo Braves, who lost the flip that year, grabbed Bob McAdoo with the second selection. Enough said.

This time Portland considered its biggest need to be at center. Paxson had made second-team All-NBA in '83–84, and Drexler, though unimpressive that season as a rookie, remained a key figure in Portland's plans. High-scoring forward Kiki Vandeweghe had just arrived from the Denver Nuggets in a momentous four-player deal. So while gambling on the injury-prone Bowie looks ridiculous in retrospect, at the time the decision made perfect sense to the Trail Blazers.

Unlike the Bulls, Portland was sound. It had gone 48–34 in 1983–84, but it hadn't had a capable pivotman since Bill Walton left after the 1977–78 season. Bowie, assuming he stayed healthy and lived up to the potential he had shown at Kentucky, was to be the final link to another title run. At least that's how Jack Ramsay, Portland's coach at the time, and general manager Stu Inman saw it.

"Our needs were obvious," says Inman now. "To have a shot at going all the way, we had to find rebounding help. We had to draft for size and intimidation. Bowie provided all of that."

"I had gone to Bowie's hometown, Lebanon, Pennsylvania, to work him out," recalls Ramsay. "I worked him out myself, just the two us in a local gym. I told him that unless something crazy happened, we were going to take him with the second pick. I showed him some things I wanted him to improve on over the summer and said that I'd see him in training camp.

"We had Paxson and Drexler. We needed a big man. No one knew Michael Jordan was going to become the greatest player to play the game. Nobody."

Not exactly. Although Thorn and most every other member of the Bull organization admits to having had no idea how good Jordan would become, the skinny had started to emerge from members of the '84 Olympic team. Said George Raveling, an assistant coach of the U.S. team, "He does things in practice that are mind-boggling. I'd only seen Michael on TV, and I'd never gotten a true appreciation of how good he is. Down the road, I think Michael will create a tremendous controversy as to why he wasn't picked first or second in the draft."

In the days leading up to the draft, however, no one spoke of such controversy. Portland needed a big man, and Bowie made sense. So when Stern announced that Chicago had chosen Jordan, there was no celebration at the team's draft headquarters, where a modest group of locals had assembled for the event.

"They were real happy, but it wasn't like, Wow, this is it," recalls public-relations director Tim Hallam. "They thought we had picked a solid player who would turn out to be good for the team, but not the greatest player in the league. Shaquille O'Neal? Not even close. They figured we got a kid from North Carolina from Dean Smith's program, and they said Michael was a great guy. No, the atmosphere around the draft was nothing like when Shaquille or [New York Knick center] Patrick Ewing [was drafted]."

With the Olympic team sequestered in Indianapolis for practices, Jordan remembers the moment passing quickly. He did his little bit for the press and called his family, which had hosted a huge party for friends back in Wilmington. "The day he was picked, I was working and they let me off early," says Michael's father, James. "A television station actually came and set up in our living room. My wife, Deloris, was working at the bank, and she got off early too. So the whole family was home sitting there in front of the camera.

"We had an idea of what was going to happen, but everyone knows that on draft day a lot of deals can happen. So it was quite interesting to see if the whole scenario would be played out the way we thought it would. Michael called right after they called his name. He was excited and we were excited. We had the biggest party ever in the neighborhood that night. It was tremendous. Everybody came over and carried our privacy home with them."

Recalls Michael, "There had been some disagreements about whether the Bulls should take me, so when they picked me I was happy. I had never even been to Chicago. I didn't know anything about the city, nothing. I didn't know anything about the team except that it was bad. I didn't know any of the players, any of the past players, nothing. I didn't know much about the NBA at all."

Jordan pauses and says, "It really is funny how things turn out." ■

Mike Dunleavy gave Jordan the Olympian a taste of the pros.

CARL SKALAK

THE BEST DEFENSE AGAINST MURPHY'S LAW.

If it can go wrong, it will. From a major piece of equipment to something small that still manages to foul up the works. That's when Grainger rushes to your defense.

THE RIGHT STUFF.

We stock over 42,000 essential items for your business, plant or job. Ladders to light-bulbs, buckets to bits.

RIGHT HERE.

Grainger's as close as your phone. Day or night. One of our 335 branches is probably just a few minutes away.

RIGHT NOW.

By the time you get here, we'll have your order ready. Or we can ship or deliver if you want. We strive to get your order in your hands the fastest and easiest way. And that's Grainger's Law. *For a free catalog, call: 1-800-473-3473.*

The Right Stuff. Right Here. Right Now.®

1991

1

Jerry Krause

STEPS TO THE TOP

Despite already having the greatest player in history, the Chicago Bulls needed a grand plan to become the best

BY RICK TELANDER

JOHN W. MCDONOUGH

In the midst of one of those blowouts of another hapless foe by the Bulls, here's what you start to think about: What if 11 of the 12 Bulls took showers and the team became just you, three other guys from the stands and Michael. How about it? You'd cruise to the W. No question.

It doesn't take much skill to cling to Superman's cape, you reason. Play a little D, set a pick or two, give the rock to MJ and watch the overhead scoreboard explode. Right?

Maybe not.

Probably not.

No chance.

Playing with the greatest player of all time can't be as easy as it looks from the mezzanine. If it were, Chicago would have nine championship trophies by now rather than three, and former Bulls like Steve Johnson, Orlando Woolridge, Caldwell Jones and Ennis Whatley would be smoking victory cigars. Those four players were Jordan's opening-day sidemen during his rookie season, 1984–85, and they rode Superman's draft all the way to a 38–44 record.

Critics say the Bulls without Jordan are the Charlotte Hornets. "It would be an accomplishment if this team, without Jordan, even made the playoffs," says former Portland Trail Blazer coach Jack Ramsay, who's currently an ESPN analyst. He may be right, but here's the catch—this team was put together *to* play with Jordan.

For the record, Jordan's accomplices in the starting lineup this season were forwards Horace Grant and Scottie Pippen, center Bill Cartwright and guard B.J. Armstrong. Throw in veteran guard and previous starter John Paxson, and you have a supporting quintet that has been together for four years, 295 victories, three NBA crowns and two million "What's it like playing with Michael?" questions. The answer? "Amazing," says Paxson, speaking for all.

But if you think it's easy being one of these guys, living your life holding somebody else's silk robe, just ask Lady Di how

BILL SMITH

TOM LYNN

much fun she had all those years standing behind Prince Chuck (the one from London, not Phoenix).

No, the Bulls did not materialize by accident. Everything had to be accounted for—positions, skills, egos—and then the mix had to be made palatable to His Airness. Jordan destroyed forward Brad Sellers, Chicago's first-round pick in 1986, body and soul because he found Sellers too sugary. As late as the 1986–87 season the Bulls were still decidedly mediocre. They finished 40–42, but the recipe for success lay on the counter.

Says former NBA coach Dick Versace, "To get the team to its current level, Bull management had a plan arrived at through reaction and pro-action." Reaction, says Versace, meant that general manager Jerry Krause reacted to the stiffs on the team and dumped them. Pro-action? "That means they got Pippen and the other guys," says Versace. O.K.

In fact, Chicago took 10 precise steps of action—re-, pro- and otherwise—since owner Jerry Reinsdorf purchased the team in March 1985 with Jordan already aboard and the NBA title nowhere in sight. Each was essential to the Bulls' success. Think of Jordan as prime rib and the 10 steps as spices, silverware, fine wine, soft music, etc. We, of course, are the lucky diners.

Minor Minutes, Major Shots

John Paxson had showered and dressed and was on his way out the door of the visitors' locker room at the America West Arena shortly after Game 2 of this year's championship series when a camera crew caught up with him. Moments later a knot of reporters had crowded around him, and Paxson stood near the door and patiently answered questions, his plans for a quick escape having been foiled. It's not that Paxson was avoiding the press; it's just that he has come to make a habit out of arriving, getting the job done efficiently and slipping away quietly.

His Game 2 performance was a perfect example of what coach Phil Jackson has come to ask of the 6′ 2″ guard. He played only 12 minutes and made two just field goals, but they were crucial minutes and clutch baskets in the Bulls' 111–108 win. "That's typical Pax," says Michael Jordan. "He has a knack of hitting that shot that breaks the other team's back."

None was more backbreaking than Paxson's three-pointer with 3.9 seconds remaining in Game 6, which helped clinch the Bulls' third straight title.

In past years Paxson, 32, was more than a spot player. Last season he was Jordan's partner in the backcourt, averaging 24.6 minutes and 7.0 points. However, off-season surgery on his left knee—he also missed 22 games after undergoing arthroscopic surgery on the same knee in February—and the emergence of B.J. Armstrong combined to force Paxson to the bench for most of this season. His playing time fell to 17.5 minutes per game and his scoring average to 4.2 points, and he had some difficulty adjusting to life as a substitute.

"Some guys are good at coming off the bench with instant offense, but I'm not that type; I'm too old and too slow," says Paxson with a smile. "But I slowly started to get the hang of it."

Three NBA titles are proof of that. "One reason we've been able to do what we've done is that not only do we all believe in ourselves, but we also have confidence in each other," Paxson says. "We play well together because every player on this team has complete faith that every other player will do his job well, no matter how big or small that job is." —PHIL TAYLOR

4 John Paxson

BILL SMITH

1) *On March 26, 1985, 13 days after buying the Bulls, Reinsdorf hires Krause.*

Krause, a rotund and obsessive former scout and executive with Reinsdorf's Chicago White Sox and other major league teams, replaced Rod Thorn. Krause, who covets draftable sports talent the way a gerbil covets seeds, promptly tried to figure out how to improve a team that already had one great player as well as some of the strangest. "What a group," says Krause now, still quaking. There were mercurial 7-footer Jawann Oldham, awkward Mike Smrek (as in wreck) and drug-abuser Quintin Dailey, among others.

"I knew that with Jordan we'd never be bad enough to get a great center in the draft," says Krause. "And we were trying to build a championship team around a two guard, which had never been done before. So this was going to be tough."

He made the decision to find players to complement Jordan, not rival him. If he couldn't get an All-Star center, he would at least pursue shorter players who were quick, tough defenders, solid citizens and good shooters. "We have to have a shooter at every position," Krause once said. "Otherwise Michael will get doubled to death."

BILL SMITH

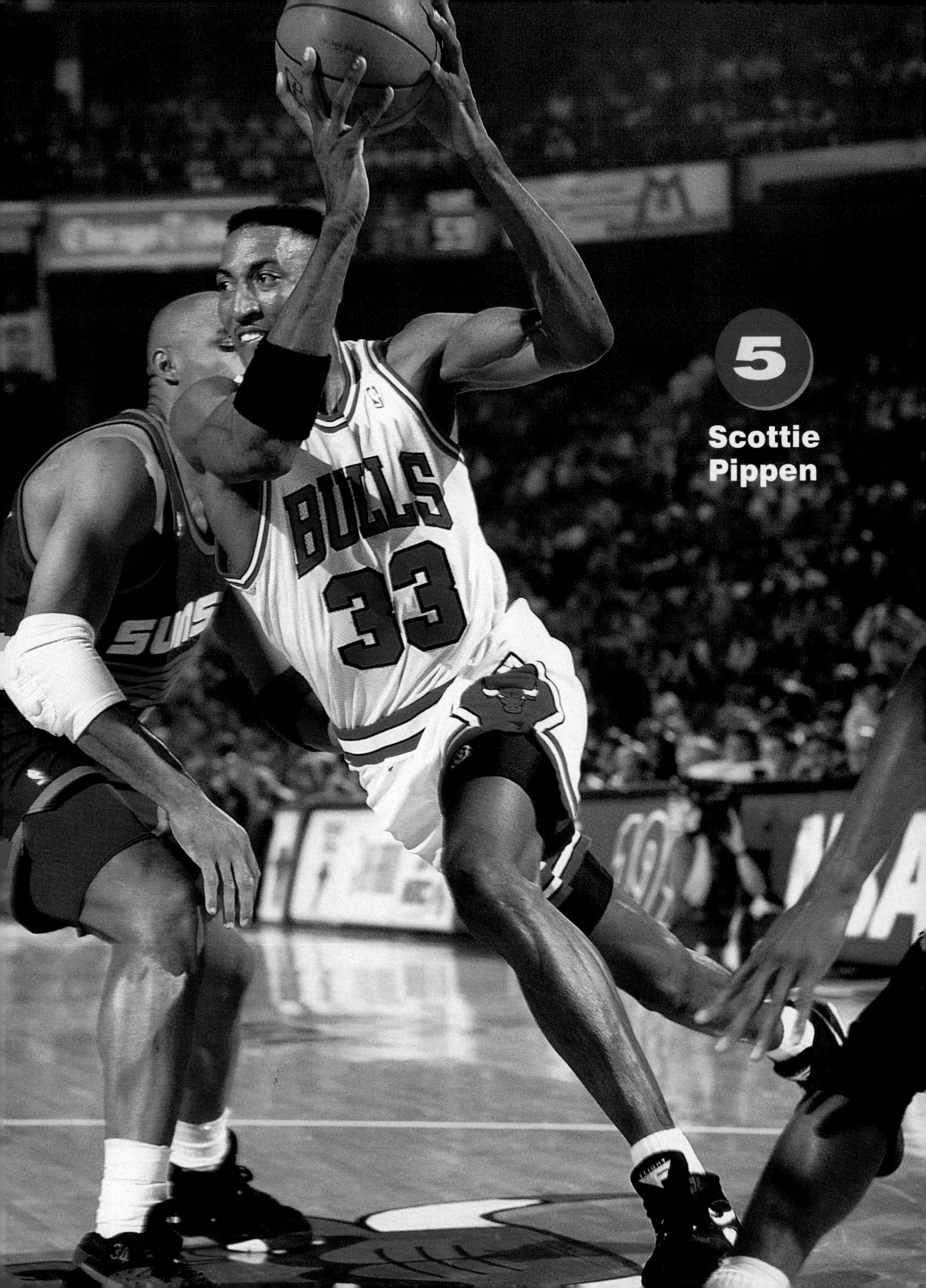

5

Scottie Pippen

"I've Learned a Lot"

JOHN W. MCDONOUGH

The opening game of the '93 Finals is 90 minutes away, and Horace Grant is stretched out in front of his locker in the America West Arena, reading a *U.S. News & World Report* story about South Central Los Angeles one year after the riots there. When a reporter asks about his pending task—guarding Charles Barkley—Grant marks his place with a finger, looks up, answers the question, then resumes reading as the reporter departs.

"I like learning about people," Grant says. "Playing basketball is one thing. But people in different situations, different worlds, that's what is really intriguing."

Even 90 minutes before the NBA Finals? "Well," says Grant with a laugh, "I've learned a lot in these last three years. In the first championship, I was like a little kid; it was new, thrilling. The second year I was more mature, so there was a little more pressure. The third? Well, now I'm an adult. I know how to prepare."

If that preparation includes increasing your knowledge of world events while your teammates are getting taped, so be it. Who's to argue with success? Grant, 28, played an integral role in all three championships. Over that span he was the team's leading rebounder with 9.3 per game and ranked third in scoring—behind the big two—with 13.4 points per game.

Moreover, with his massive strength under the basket, the 6′ 10″ Grant has helped transform the position of power forward. "He is the quickest forward in the league," says center Bill Cartwright, "and when he added the muscle, he became one of the strongest."

The muscle didn't come for a couple of years. When the Bulls made Grant the 10th pick in the 1987 draft, he was a 200-pounder from Clemson. Eventually he grew tired of the incessant batterings he was taking and started training with the Bulls' strength coaches. Soon he weighed 235 pounds, which meant fans could finally tell the difference between Horace and twin brother Harvey, who was traded to the Portland Trail Blazers on June 24. Horace is the one with biceps.

Grant changed his off-court M.O., too. Three years ago he joined the Pentecostal Church and began reading the Bible instead of closing clubs. He and Scottie Pippen had been famous around town for their late-night exploits, but Grant tired of the life-style and set about becoming what he calls "a better person." The two players have somewhat drifted apart.

"It's been an interesting year," says Grant. "There's been a lot of controversy, but I guess it's all worked out. I've learned a lot."

Especially about people. —SHELLEY SMITH

2) *On June 18, 1985, the Bulls acquire Charles Oakley.*

Krause, who had often stated that he wanted only "athletes" on his team, promptly went out and snared the 6′ 9″ Oakley in a draft-day swap with the Cleveland Cavaliers. In return the Cavs got Whatley and frail rookie Keith Lee. Oakley turned out to be a bruising hulk whose main skills were yanking down rebounds and acting mean. "I took Oakley because the team was soft," says Krause. "He started our toughness."

Oakley became Jordan's bodyguard, Marty McSorley to Wayne Gretzky. In time he would serve an even larger function in the building of the team.

3) *On Aug. 1, 1985, the Bulls hire Al Vermeil to be their strength-and-conditioning coach.*

That's right, the brother of famous burnt-out NFL coach Dick Vermeil has helped transform the Bulls from a weak bunch into a fit bunch. Although the Bulls don't have the bulk of, say, the Knicks, they have the fibrous strength of a pack of Dobermans. And it shows in their defense and their fourth-quarter fire, much of which can be attributed to Vermeil's program. A former strength coach for the San Francisco 49ers, Vermeil has an NFL championship ring to go with his three from the NBA.

4) *On Oct. 29, 1985, the Bulls get Paxson.*

Paxson, who had played the previous two seasons with the San Antonio Spurs before becoming a free agent, is not a star, nor will he ever be, but he works hard, says little and can bury the J. Just ask the Phoenix Suns.

As a starter in 1991–92, Paxson led all point guards in field goal percentage and had the fewest turnovers. Now, as a sub for Armstrong, he gives the ball to Jordan and then hangs near the three-point line in case Jordan gets into trouble and needs a bailout man. It was during Chicago's first title run, against the Los Angeles Lakers in the 1991 Finals, that Paxson's worth became obvious to all.

"Who's open?" coach Phil Jackson asked a frustrated Jordan during a time-out in Game 5.

"Paxson," answered Jordan.

Jordan passed off, and Paxson finished with 20 points, including 10 in the last four minutes. Jordan had 10 assists.

Old but Not Obsolete

Bill Cartwright is the grand Bull. He is stoic and soft-spoken, a 7-footer who is all elbows. Over the years this grizzled warrior with the quirky shot has taken on younger, stronger, quicker and meaner opponents and outlasted them despite injuries and chronic pain. These days, though, he's just a big guy who is sick of talking about his age and his throbbing knees and about whether he can play a few more seasons.

"I'm as fit as a fiddle," says Cartwright, who will turn 36 on July 30. He pauses and then corrects himself: "No, wait. I'm as fit as a Kentucky racehorse."

His eyes dance mischievously as a half-smile flits across his face and fades. "Well, some days I am," he says.

JOHN W. MCDONOUGH

After 14 pro seasons, Cartwright is nursing-home material by NBA standards. The flecks of gray in his goatee, not to mention the perfect white circle that suddenly appeared there several years ago, only add to Cartwright's image as an ancient mariner. He knows his playing days are numbered. In fact, the Bulls have the option to buy out his contract for the 1993–94 season for $800,000—a slot that apparently has been slated for European star Toni Kukoc. But general manager Jerry Krause must consider this: For three years the Bulls have withstood assaults from the league's premier pivotmen, and Cartwright is the primary reason.

"No question about it," said forward Horace Grant. "We wouldn't be here without Bill."

In 1988 Cartwright was traded to the Bulls for forward Charles Oakley, a move most Chicago fans—and some players—greeted with disgust: a 24-year-old for a 30-year-old. In time, Cartwright proved he could still hang with the youngsters. "It was a long time until I felt like I fit in here," he says, "but, personally, I was happy because I was playing a lot more. Gradually, things got better."

So did Chicago, thanks in no small part to the grand Bull. —S.S.

And Chicago finally had its crown.

5) *On June 22, 1987, the Bulls acquire Pippen.*

Here was the maniacally secretive Krause at his best—scouting, spying, calculating, dissembling, acting, wheeling and dealing—all so he could land this 6′ 7″ diamond in the rough from NAIA Central Arkansas in the 1987 draft. Krause had taken one look at Pippen in a predraft camp, had seen that he could shoot and jump and had "arms down to his toes," and had gone after him like a hound after a rabbit. The Bulls, who had the eighth pick in the draft, gave the Seattle SuperSonics the rights to that pick, plus a second-round selection in 1988 or 1989, as well as other considerations, for the rights to Seattle's first-round choice. Seattle, which had the fifth pick, selected Pippen for the Bulls; Krause took forward Olden Polynice of Virginia for the Sonics. Guess who got the better deal.

When paired with Jordan on a full-court press or a fast break, Pippen becomes part of the most explosive midsize tandem ever to play the game. A member of the NBA's All-Defensive team at small forward each of the last two years, Pippen is harder to get past than Spider-Man.

But like all the other Bulls, Pippen simply fits in. The ego is in check. When asked on a Bull profile sheet if he would share one random thought with the public, Pippen wrote, "Give and you will receive." Give to Michael and receive rings in return.

6) *On June 22, 1987, the Bulls draft Grant.*

Taken in the same draft that produced Pippen, the 6′ 10″ Grant is the power forward who helped cement Krause's coronation as 1987–88 NBA Executive of the Year. And just think, Krause had to be talked out of drafting North Carolina's Joe Wolf by Doug Collins, Chicago's coach at the time.

Grant's athletic ability allows him to run with Jordan and Pippen, and his strength and work ethic have made him the team's leading rebounder.

Sometimes the usually agreeable Grant gets perturbed enough with his low-scoring (13.2 points per game during the 1992–93 regular season), lunch-bucket role to lash out at his higher-profile buddies. "I've even thought about stealing the ball from Scottie or Michael so I can take

8

B.J. Armstrong

JOHN W. MCDONOUGH

Not Just a Baby Face

It is his face, round and smooth, with eyes as wide and soft as a child's, that gives the impression that B.J. Armstrong is fragile and easily bruised. But if Armstrong were as sensitive as he looks, he never could have withstood the questions that arose when he replaced John Paxson as Michael Jordan's backcourt partner early in the season. The Bulls struggled for awhile, and some critics pointed to the most obvious difference—Armstrong's increased playing time.

"That experience definitely made me a better player because I had to find strength somewhere within me to take the criticism for what it was worth and turn it into a challenge," he says. "When you go through some tough times and survive them, you come out stronger."

Armstrong went on to finish the regular season as the team's fourth leading scorer (12.3 points per game), and he saved some of his finest moments for the playoffs. The biggest may have been the three-pointer he drained against the New York Knicks in the final 1:17 of the fifth game of the Eastern Conference finals, which swung the series in Chicago's favor for good. But the biggest contribution Armstrong made in the postseason came on defense, helping to bottle up Mookie Blaylock of the Atlanta Hawks, Mark Price of the Cleveland Cavaliers, John Starks of New York and Kevin Johnson of the Phoenix Suns.

"Here's a headline for you: B.J. AGAINST KJ WAS A-OK," said forward-center Stacey King during the '93 Finals. "We knew coming into the series that stopping KJ's penetration, or at least cutting it down, was essential if we were going to win."

The championship is all the sweeter for Armstrong because of those bitter moments early this season, which he survived with the help of assistant coach Jim Cleamons and veteran teammate Trent Tucker. "There's a saying: That which does not kill us makes us stronger," Tucker says. "B.J. learned the meaning of that this year. He's grown up a lot in the last eight or nine months."

More than anything, though, Armstrong credits his success to the amount of playing time he received as a starter. "This year was the first time I was ever asked to go out and guard someone like Mark Price for 30 minutes," he says. "In the past my job was to come in as a reserve and create havoc during certain stretches of the game, but this year it was to do a solid defensive job from beginning to end. The more that was asked of me, I think, the better I became."

Armstrong and the rest of the Bulls expect Armstrong's improvement to continue, although he knows that his innocent looks will always belie his inner strength. "Maybe I wouldn't be tested so much by other teams if I had a nastier look," he says, "but I'll never have a Charles Barkley kind of face. People have always gotten the wrong impression by looking at my face."

Maybe now his critics will realize that the place to look for insights into Armstrong is not his face but his hand—the one with the three rings. —P.T.

A Few Good Men

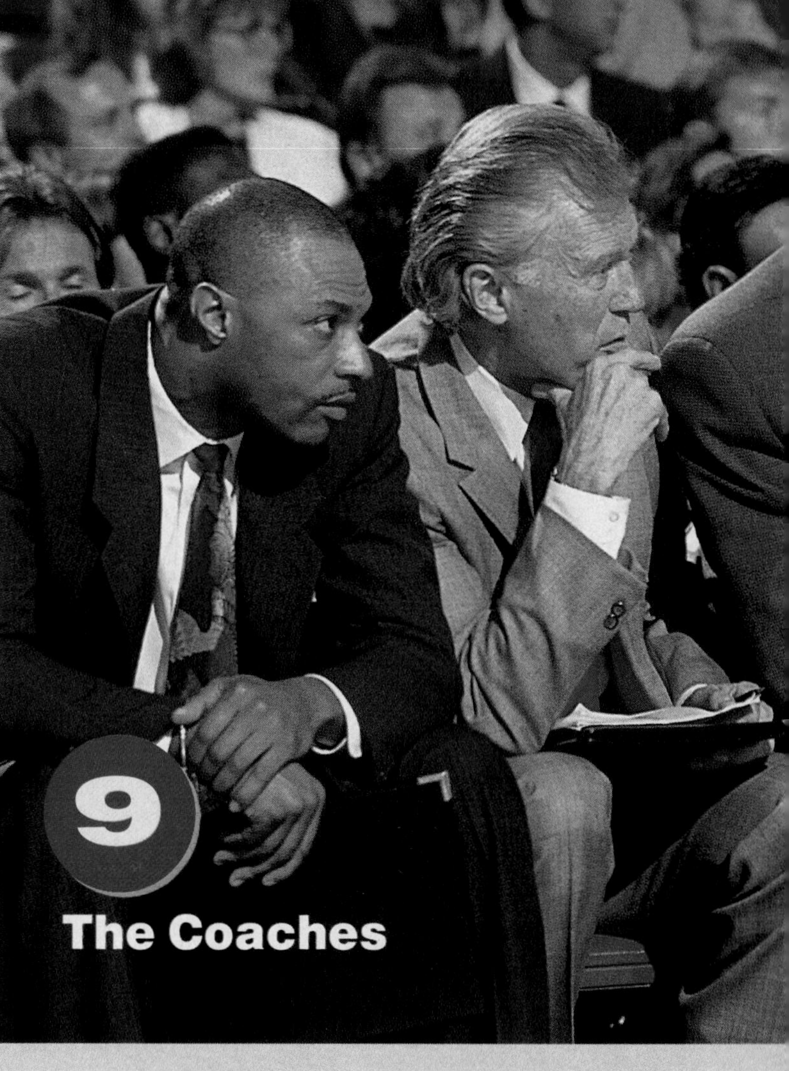

Assistant coach John Bach, a former naval officer and a student of all things military, can make a trip to the grocery store sound like the invasion of Normandy. Usually, Bach's warlike metaphors are perfectly appropriate. It's fitting, for instance, that he refers to himself and his fellow assistants, Tex Winter and Jim Cleamons, as coach Phil Jackson's lieutenants, because when they meet at about 8 a.m. on the day of a home game at the Berto Center, the room becomes a command center where they help Jackson prepare his troops for battle.

Bach *(second from left)* constructs the defense, which he once described as "fortifying the citadel to withstand enemy assault." Winter *(far right)*, the offensive guru, suggests creative ways to deploy such smart bombs as Michael Jordan and Scottie Pippen. Cleamons *(far left)* scouts the enemy, er, opponent.

Their responsibilities may neatly mesh, but Bach, Winter and Cleamons are an unlikely mix. "Some people look at us and say this is a strange brew," says Bach, 67. "You've got Tex and myself, two opinionated guys who have been in coaching so long that a lot of people think of us as dinosaurs. You've got Jim, who's the opposite of us in that he's more of a strong, silent type. Then you have Phil, who's been known to apply Zen teachings to the game, play Pink Floyd to the team and bring incense into the locker room. I'm sure some people would look at this staff and say, What in the world is going on there?"

Bach is also in charge of most of the tape editing, a job he attacks far more creatively than most coaches. "John likes to slip scenes from war movies into our tapes," says center Bill Cartwright. "We might be ready to watch films of the Knicks' trap, and suddenly we're looking at a scene from *Apocalypse Now*."

Parts of such movies as *A Few Good Men*, *An Officer and a Gentleman* and *Full Metal Jacket* have all been screened by the Bulls. "I'll use any scene that illustrates something we're looking for—leadership, responsibility, loyalty," says Bach, whose highest form of congratulations to a player after a good game is not a high five but a salute. "It's not that I think the world should go military; it's just that there are some values you learn there that we would do well to apply to sport and life in general."

Bach has been coaching for 42 years—he held head-coaching jobs at Fordham and Penn State and with the Golden State Warriors—but that's not tops on the staff. That distinction belongs to the 70-year-old Winter, who has 46 years of experience, a span

a shot," he told an interviewer last fall. In the end, though, he always chills and returns to business.

7) *On June 27, 1988, the Bulls trade for Cartwright.*

Getting the ungainly Mr. Bill from the Knicks in a trade for Oakley was the move that put Chicago over the top. Krause and the coaching staff had decided that the summit was unattainable with the current center, Dave Corzine, and that it might be sometime in the next century before the team could draft a young stud who could blossom in the middle. So when New York came knocking for a power forward to assist Patrick Ewing, the Bulls tossed out the supposedly untouchable Oakley and scarfed up Cartwright—bad foot, sharp elbows, corkscrew shot and all.

"Picking Scottie was a great thing," says longtime Bull analyst and former head coach John Kerr. "And getting Horace at that spot was great too. But both those things were logical. Getting Bill was the big move. It made the difference."

It was made possible by a chain reaction of good fortune. Krause had hired Vermeil, who had built up Grant, who was now sturdy enough to replace Oakley, who had protected Jordan, who was to be

BILL SMITH

ments," says Winter. "They're more like heated debates."

Observing all of this is Cleamons, 43, who is every bit as intense as his colleagues but tends to keep his emotions in check. "In his quiet way Jim has learned to live with us," says Bach. "There is a fire smoldering in him."

Cleamons, a veteran of nine seasons with the Los Angeles Lakers, the Cleveland Cavaliers, the New York Knicks, and the Washington Bullets, considers working with Jackson, Winter and Bach the ideal apprenticeship. "It's like working with three distinguished professors in graduate school," says Cleamons, who spends almost as much time watching other teams as he does his own.

Cleamons's tenure with Chicago might be his last step on the way to an NBA head-coaching job. He is the only one of the assistants with that aspiration. That's not a coincidence. In fact, the presence of Bach and Winter may represent the start of a trend in which NBA coaches with little head-coaching experience hire more-experienced men as assistants, both because of their tenure in the league and because they have no designs on the head job.

that includes five college head-coaching jobs (Marquette, Kansas State, Washington, Northwestern and Long Beach State) and one in the NBA (the San Diego/Houston Rockets).

Winter has long been respected as one of the game's finest offensive minds—his triangle offense is the foundation of the Bulls' attack—yet he also admits to being something of an absent-minded professor. "I might have a hard time remembering the name of someone I met two hours ago," says Winter, "but I remember every player I've ever been associated with."

With 88 years of experience between them, it's not surprising that Winter and Bach have strong opinions on the game and that those opinions aren't always compatible. "We don't have argu-

"I think you're going to see it more and more," says Bach. "Teams are hiring more guys not far removed from their playing careers to be head coaches, and they're surrounding them with people who can give them the benefit of more years of experience without being a threat. Tex and I are content. We've had our time in the spotlight. Maybe that's why this staff gets along so well."

Or maybe it's because they have been through so much together. As Bach would surely tell you, this staff is like any good platoon: The most important thing is not that its members have different backgrounds, temperaments and opinions but that they would trust one another in a foxhole. —P.T.

the beneficiary of it all. Cartwright, expected to provide scoring relief for Jordan, turned out to be a defensive ace. His scoring average has declined steadily since he arrived in Chicago—12.4 points per game in 1988–89 to 5.6 this season—but his ability to harass opposing pivotmen has freed his teammates to play their own gambling, frenzied defense without worrying about helping in the middle.

Beyond that, Cartwright is a calming influence on his sometimes hyper teammates. He is, as *Chicago Tribune* writer Don Pierson put it, "the team's anchor, its link to reality." What's more, he is now a man of history, having joined George Mikan and Bill Russell as the only starting centers to win three straight world titles.

8) *On June 27, 1989, the Bulls draft Armstrong.*

Armstrong at first appeared to be a clueless, baby-faced point guard who would soon be establishing himself with the Topeka Sizzlers. Why did Krause take him? "Because I liked his shooting," says Krause. "I wanted another Paxson."

Once Armstrong realized the Bulls don't really have a point guard in their offense, he started to figure out that standing calmly behind the three-point stripe

JOHN W. MCDONOUGH

and burying wide-open treys might be a way for him, like Paxson, to make his mark. This season, his first as a starter, Armstrong led the league in three-point shooting percentage (.453). And, wouldn't you know it—as Krause says—"B.J. is really a great person, too."

9) *On July 10, 1989, the Bulls promote Jackson from assistant to head coach, the first move toward building a good coaching staff.*

In his nine seasons with Chicago, Jordan has played for Kevin Loughery, Stan Albeck, Doug Collins and now Jackson. Each of them has taught him something different, but each has also learned from the star. Jackson, who followed the successful but overly intense Collins, has the kind of laid-back, off-the-wall demeanor that seems appropriate for a team that needs soothing more than it needs firing up. He learned from Collins's mistakes.

Then, too, there are the Bulls' three assistant coaches—Jim Cleamons and a pair of wise senior citizens, Tex Winter and John Bach. The last two offer a sort of reassuring counterpoint in a vicious world where old age starts at 30.

10) *The Bulls acquire a decent bench.*

This season it consisted of Will Perdue (drafted June 28, 1988), Stacey King (drafted June 27, 1989), Scott Williams (signed as a free agent on July 25, 1990), Rodney McCray (obtained in a trade Sept. 18, 1992), Trent Tucker (signed as a free agent Oct. 5, 1992) and Darrell Walker (signed as a free agent Jan. 28, 1993). They are good practice players, and they have good attitudes. As Tucker, who was acquired for his long-range shooting, puts it, "It doesn't have to be stated; everybody knows who the man is."

The bench changes often, but one thing remains the same. "The guys they bring in have character," says King. They have to, or else Jordan will turn them to jelly.

"He just kills guys," says Krause. "People wonder why I don't bring in a young two guard to work under Michael. I can't. Michael wrecks whoever is across from him in practice. A kid can't handle that."

Those are the 10 basic steps that took the Bulls to the top, though there were plenty of little shuffles that also contributed. For example, says Cartwright, "getting beat up by Detroit all those years really helped us grow."

But the team's development went mostly according to plan. Nothing was guaranteed. With bad moves and bad luck and bad teammates, Jordan could have ended up like Chicago's favorite great loser, Ernie Banks.

"Sometimes I wonder what it would have been like if I'd gone to a lousy team where I started right away," says King, no doubt speaking for a number of his fellow subs. He ponders this a moment and then smiles. "But here I have three rings. I'm a piece of the puzzle. Not a big piece, but a piece. And it feels good." ■

MANNY MILLAN

MICHAEL

in MOTION

ANDREW D. BERNSTEIN/NBA PHOTOS

BULLS
23
00

NATHANIEL BUTLER

BILL SMITH

ANDREW D. BERNSTEIN/NBA PHOTOS

SAN ANTONIO SPURS
BUD LIGHT
diet Coke

MANNY MILLAN

BULLS
23
PHILADELP
SIXERS
33

NATHANIEL BUTLER/NBA PHOTOS

MANNY MILLAN

THAT CHAMPIONSHIP SEASON

1

that he had scored two points on one-for-10 shooting and had four rebounds. The Bulls lost again.

Two points? In the biggest game of his life? A migraine headache?

"How do you explain the things that happen?" Pippen asks. "The time against Laimbeer, I wanted to go back. I asked and asked to go back. The doctors and [Bull general manager] Jerry Krause wouldn't let me. I'd never had a migraine before. It's very hard to tell people what you feel like in that situation. If I were on the other side, it would be very hard to tell *me*. And once you get people on your back, it's hard to get them off."

Two games. Two nights. A reputation was born. The whisper—heck, the headline—was that Pippen was soft. He had a heart the consistency of oleomargarine, not even real butter. Push him, and he would go down and not come back. Turn on the gas-station air pump, get the bells ringing, and the increased pressure would make him fall apart. Soft. Soft. Soft. Pippen? Very good on a January night in, say, Dallas, against the Mavericks. Put him in a postseason sweatbox, though, winner takes all, championships and money at stake, and where will he be? Sitting on the bench under an ice pack.

It did not matter that Krause, for one, backed Pippen's story of the Laimbeer night. The doctor had unequivocally stated to Krause that Pippen should not return to the game. What was Krause going to do? Go against the doctor? And it did not matter that various migraine specialists publicly detailed the pain and effects of a withering headache. The casual observer only had to look farther along the Bulls' bench to see how a champion should perform. Look at Jordan. When the going gets tough and all of that. Jordan had no migraines. Jordan had no knockout blows delivered to his head.

A pleasant basketball story suddenly had turned sour. Soft. That was the only word Pippen could hear. How could he rewind the reels? How could he start the movie again? Just the picture of him, often wearing wire-rim glasses that gave him the appearance of a successful young scholar or account executive, seemed to be an indictment. Soft. The way he played, graceful and controlled, soaring over and around other people, never muscling through them, was a second indictment. Indictments were everywhere. No matter where he went or what he did, he was trailed by the memories of those two nights. How do you change public opinion? How do you change what so many people have decided is true?

A reputation was born. The whisper—the headline—was Pippen was soft.

That was Pippen's challenge. Luckily, he had experience.

"We used to play at the Pine Street courts," Ron Martin, a friend of Pippen's, says. "We must have been 13, 14, 15 years old. We'd play as late as we could, until the old man would run us off for making noise. We'd play everything. Scottie was the Giants. I was the A's. We played a million games. Basketball. We'd play one-on-one forever. We were convinced that one of us was going to make it to the NBA. We just didn't know which one. I was a little bit bigger than he was, heavier, stronger, so I used to lean on him. Then . . . somehow . . . he got big on me."

The town was Hamburg, Ark., population 3,394, a quiet and peaceful stretch of Nowhere. The NBA? One local kid, Myron Jackson, had gone off and played at the University of Arkansas–Little Rock in '82 and had a tryout with the Mavericks in

JOHN W. MCDONOUGH

Time and again Pippen has risen to the occasion.

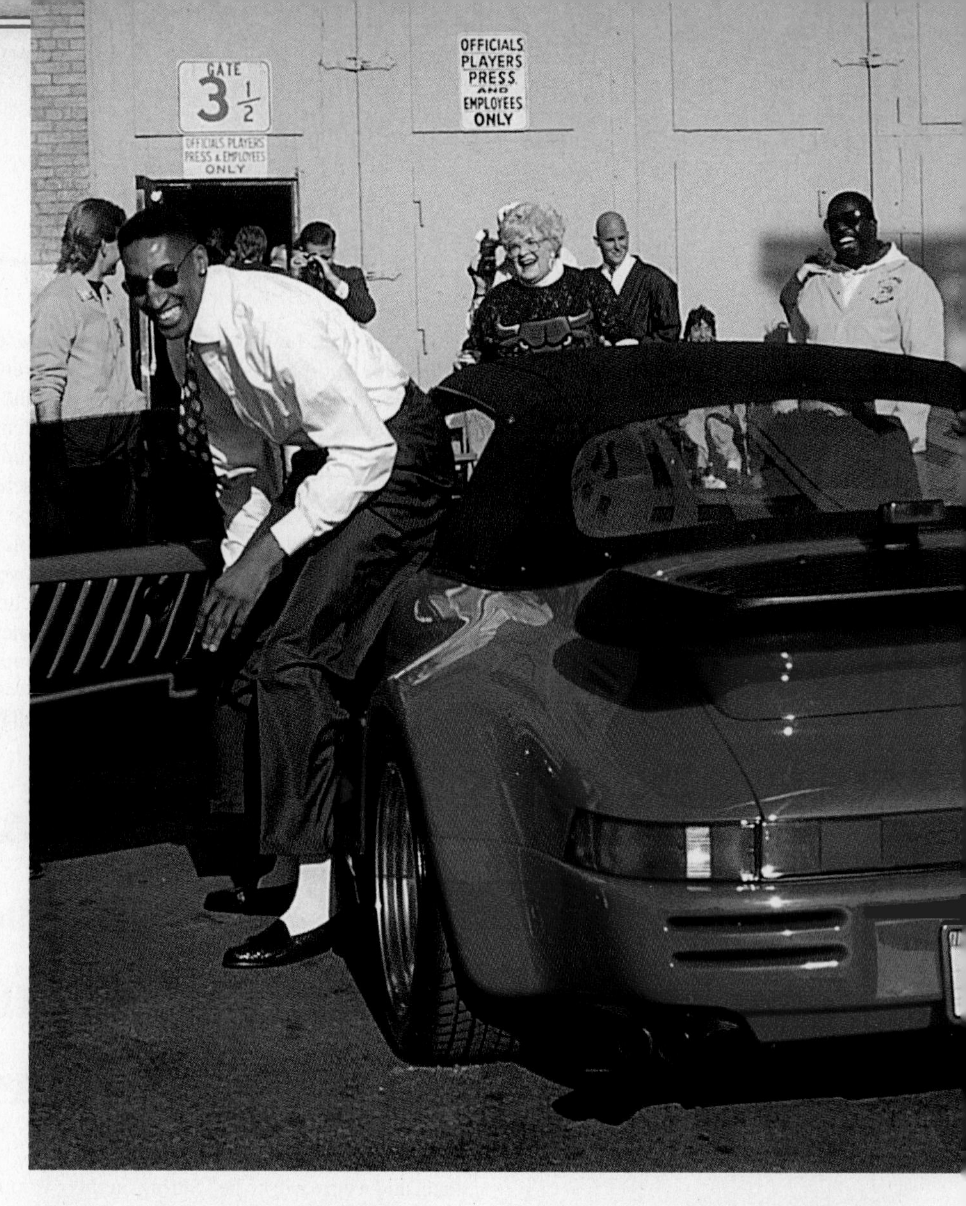

'86, but that was it for bright lights. Pippen was not exceptional. He was another good, quiet kid, moving through high school. He was 6′ 1½″ as a senior, starting at point guard. Martin, his friend, was a junior shooting guard. Donald Wayne, the coach, remembers that Pippen was "nothing tremendous, but good. Not flashy, but consistent." No Myron Jackson, for sure.

High school ended for Pippen without a single college offer. What to do? He asked Wayne for help. The coach says he tries to help any good kid who wants to go to college, and that was what he did for Pippen. He called Don Dyer, his old coach at Henderson State in Arkadelphia, who had moved along to the University of Central Arkanas in Conway. Wayne's promises were minimal. He said he had a point guard, 6′ 1½″, who would be a good manager under a work-study program and, well, the kid came from a big family, youngest of 12, and the parents and the brothers and sisters did seem to run sort of large. Maybe the kid also would grow. Maybe he even could be a player. Dyer took a chance. The kid grew.

He was 6′ 3″ by the time he arrived on the Central Arkansas campus.

He was 6′ 5″, 165 pounds, skinny as a minute, as a sophomore.

He was 6′ 6″, 185, as a junior.

He was 6′ 7″ by the end of his senior year.

The student-manager role disappeared early in Pippen's freshman year. He was scrimmaging with the team and playing well. The bigger he grew, the better he became.

"The surprising thing to me is that he never lost any of his coordination in all this growing," says Arch Jones, an assistant at Central Arkansas during Pippen's years there. "He was able to take the skills he had learned when he was smaller and use them when he was bigger. His arms are so long, his hands so big that he really plays like someone 6′ 10″, 6′ 11″."

Central Arkansas is an NAIA school, a small college, and it had never sent a basketball player to the pros. In 1979, Monte Coleman had moved along to play football for the Washington Redskins and five years later Wes Gardner had started pitching a baseball for the New York Mets, but no one from the school had advanced to the NBA. The idea that Pippen could make that jump came only in brief flashes of revelation. Hey! Hasn't this kid played every position on the court at one time or another? Hey! Isn't he dominating games? Couldn't you project that to another level? No one knew for sure, and the team did not help, falling a basket or two short every year in the last local tournament, and failing to qualify for the NAIA finals and national exposure in Kansas City.

With Jordan nagged by controversies, Pippen was a reliable antidote.

"I remember thinking at the end of his sophomore season that Scottie had a chance," Dyer says. "I'd seen Sidney Moncrief and Darrell Walker play at the University of Arkansas, and they both made it to the NBA, and I thought Scottie was bigger and better. I called San Antonio and I called Dallas, but no one seemed interested. I knew Bob Bass, then the general manager at San Antonio. I told him about Scottie. Wasn't interested. I see him now, and every time he says, 'You tried to tell me. . . .' "

"I always thought he had a chance," Jones says, "but I realized how good he was when I saw him with all of those players at the NBA tryout camp in Chicago.

The first title drive, in 1990–91, came down to a face-off between M.J. and M.J.

BY JACK McCALLUM

ANDREW D. BERNSTEIN/NBA PHOTOS

On June 3, 1990, a Sunday afternoon, Scottie Pippen had a headache. And the Bulls were still hearing about it in training camp four months later. The NBA's most famous migraine, which had limited Pippen's effectiveness and helped the Detroit Pistons embarrass Chicago 93–74 in the Eastern Conference finals, seemed an apt symbol for the can't-quite-get-over-the-hump team from the Windy City. The Bulls were weak, the Pistons were strong. The Bulls cracked under pressure, the Pistons stepped up. The Bulls didn't want to win badly enough to play hurt, the Pistons turned pain into pleasure.

Michael Jordan was exempt from the aforementioned criticisms of the Bulls, of course, but that was part of the problem. The team that showed up at training camp in October of 1990 was still Jordan and his "supporting cast," the Jordanaires as they were known throughout the league. They had the talent to turn back the Pistons, who were fresh off their second straight championship and third consecutive appearance in the Finals, but whether they had enough heart was a question mark.

Still, there was much reason for optimism. Jordan was as good as ever, having averaged a league-high 33.6 points per game in the 1989–90 season, and, boy, was he hungry for a title. Horace Grant came back to camp carrying 20 extra pounds, as well as a pair of white, high-tech prescription goggles that looked like something out of a Devo video; the former would help him in the wars underneath the basket, the latter would help him actually see the ball come off the rim. And Grant would be getting help from offensive rebounding specialist Cliff Levingston, who was added to the roster via free agency.

Best of all, Phil Jackson had a year's experience under his belt as the team's coach. Some still doubted this erstwhile creature of the '60s, but those in the Chicago organization recognized him as a competitor first and foremost, a man committed to winning.

Jackson began the 1990–91 season—how else?—by trying to convince Jordan that he had to shoot less and spread the wealth more. That idea was a hoary one around Chicago, having been advanced previously by Jackson's predecessor, Doug Collins, who was fired after the 1988–89 season. But Jackson, a master psychologist, seemed just the man to carry out the plan. He intended to do it by getting Jordan and Co. to employ assistant coach Tex Winter's triple-post offense, an attack that stresses continuity and motion rather than isolations and set-up plays for a single player. Collins had never been completely sold on the triple-post (known more popularly as "the triangle") and was consequently both unable and unwilling to sell it to his players.

The Bulls, Jordan in particular, took to the system reluctantly. Jordan was routinely spectacular, even as he reduced his scoring average as requested, but he seemed uncomfortable. He sometimes scoffed at the offense and called it "that triangle stuff." Reserve center Will Perdue, referring to the programmed movements of the triple-post, likened it to "ballroom dancing." And some players, most notably Levingston, just didn't get it at all. But Jackson was firm in his belief that the Bulls had to run some sort of offense that got everyone involved, lest they continue their pattern of playoff futility.

"No, Michael doesn't need the offense," Jackson said in December 1990. "It limits him, no doubt about it. But we've let Michael clear out and try to win it by himself, and we've come up short. So let's see if we can get other people involved in the offense."

And so the Bulls' ship sailed swiftly yet uncertainly through the regular season. The team was simply too good not to find success, but it

MANNY MILLAN

A rim with a view shows how Pippen beat Armon Gilliam of the 76ers in Round 2 of the playoffs.

Travel One
Travel One
Travel One

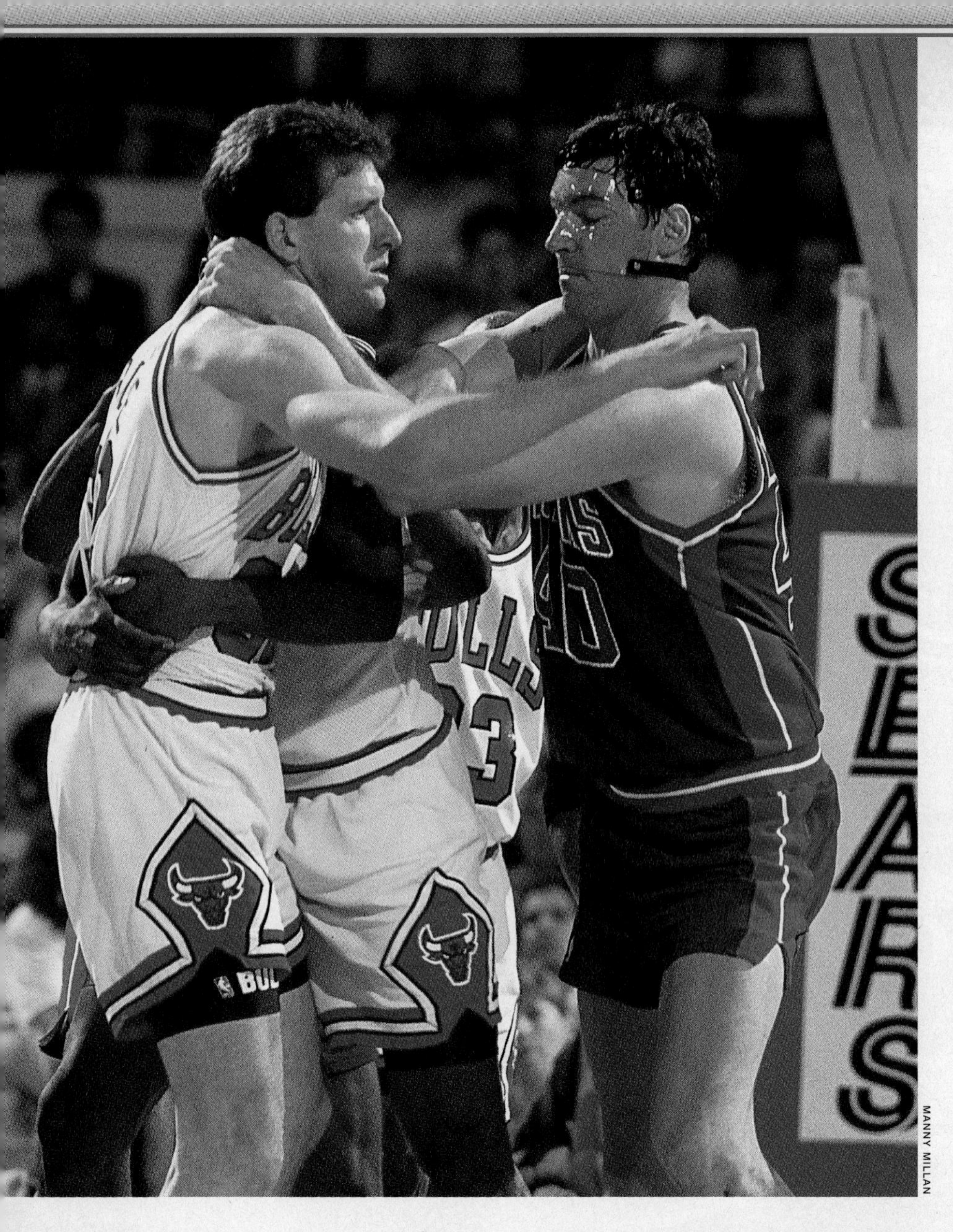

MANNY MILLAN

In an acrimonious third round, Perdue went hold-for-hold with Laimbeer (above), while Jordan went head-to-head with Dumars.

was also too adventurous not to encounter rough seas along the way. Little did the Bulls know at the time, but their proclivity for courting distractions, and for ultimately finding strength through trials, would continue over the next two seasons.

Pippen played a major role in all this. On Feb. 22 he made public his long-simmering resentment over his $765,000 salary for '90–91. He believed he was one of the league's best players and should be paid like one. He was correct about his talent, but there were those in the Bulls' front office, as well as on the Bulls' roster, who believed that he had still not sufficiently proved himself in big games. Backup center Stacey King also complained to management that he was not getting enough playing time. But Jackson handled the distractions smoothly.

Then, too, this was the season in which general manager Jerry Krause began his avid courtship of Toni Kukoc, a star player from Yugoslavia who was relatively unknown outside of Europe. As much as anything, though, Krause's pursuit of Kukoc united the Bulls. Jordan was the most vocal in expressing his opinion that the Bulls did not need Kukoc, but, in fact, no Bull wanted him. Why should they? They were playing well and wanted a chance to win a championship with the same basic group that had gone to the Eastern finals two years in a row.

With Jordan averaging "only" 31.5 points a game, good enough for his fifth straight scoring title but his lowest average since his injury-plagued second season, the Bulls finished the regular season with the league's second-best record (61–21, to the Portland Trail Blazers' 63–19) and headed into the playoffs on a high note. No one doubted that the Bulls would again make it to the conference finals, but some people doubted whether Chicago had the toughness, Jordan notwithstanding, to beat the Pistons, who had won only 50 games.

The Bulls swept the New York Knicks in the first round and lost only once while eliminating the 76ers in the best-of-seven second round. During Game 3 of that series Grant had a shouting match with Jackson after the coach criticized him for passive play. But, for once, it sounded like the truth when the Bulls blamed the flare-up on good, honest aggressiveness rather than bad team chemistry.

Meanwhile, the Pistons did indeed make it to the conference finals, though their journey was not an easy one. It was widely accepted that Detroit general manager Jack McCloskey would break up the team after the playoffs, win or lose, and no Piston was feeling too secure. Ten of the team's 12 players were 30 or over. Several players—John Salley, James Edwards and Vinnie Johnson, most notably—were complaining about their salaries, and there was the general feeling that the Pistons' physical style had taken the team about as far as it could go.

Indeed, Jackson began the psychological warfare before the series by planting the by-no-means-novel idea that the Pistons played dirty. At the same time he prepared his own team to deal with Detroit. This time the Bulls would not back down. This time they would talk a little trash and throw a few elbows in return.

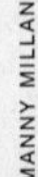
MANNY MILLAN

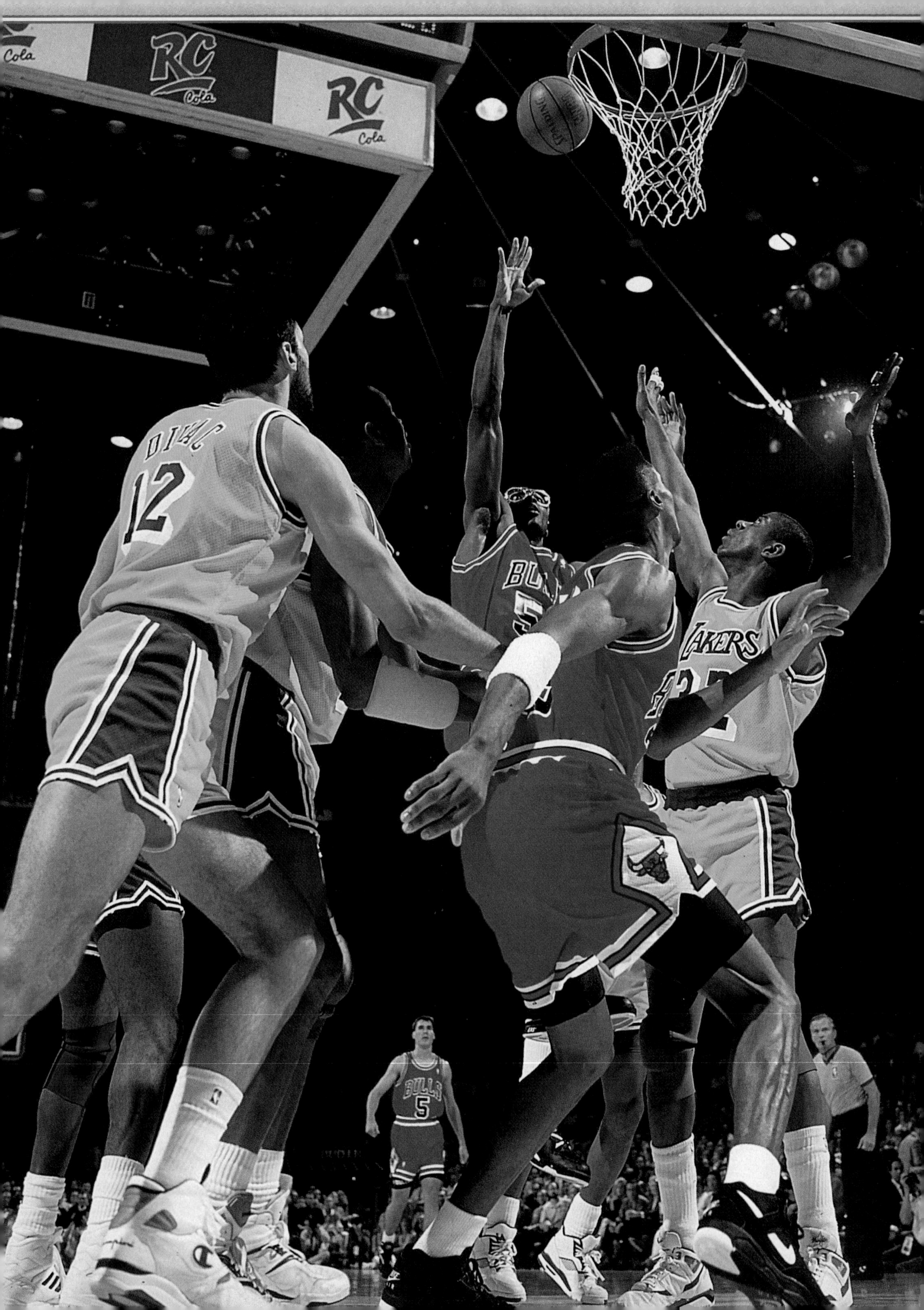
RC Cola
RC Cola
DIVAC
12
LAKERS
BULLS
5

Yet, at the same time, they would refuse to get drawn into playing Detroit's physical style. Chicago's game plan was predicated on disrupting Detroit's set-up, halfcourt offense, thus forcing the Pistons to play at an accelerated pace with which they were less comfortable.

Jackson's plan worked remarkably well. The scrambling, rambling defense that assistant coach Johnny Bach had been working to implement over the previous two seasons was finally beginning to pay off. It was a natural for the Bulls. Jordan and Pippen were solid on-the-ball defenders, but they were also good at sneaking into the passing lanes for steals. Grant was a roaming free safety, quick enough to deflect passes out front and still recover to challenge loose shooters underneath. And center Bill Cartwright and guard John Paxson were sound fundamental defenders who didn't make mistakes. Their steadiness compensated for the chances taken by Bach's "Dobermans," his term for Jordan, Pippen and Grant.

Detroit never had a chance. Just seconds before Chicago completed a four-game sweep with a 115–94 victory at the Palace of Auburn Hills (the site where Pippen had suffered his migraine a year earlier), the Pistons walked off the court. Their stated reason for the gesture was to show both team unity and their contempt for what they considered the Bulls' complaining ways. Yet the Pistons succeeded only in showing their own utter frustration and the cold, hard fact that the Bulls had clearly surpassed them as a mature, confident, championship-caliber team.

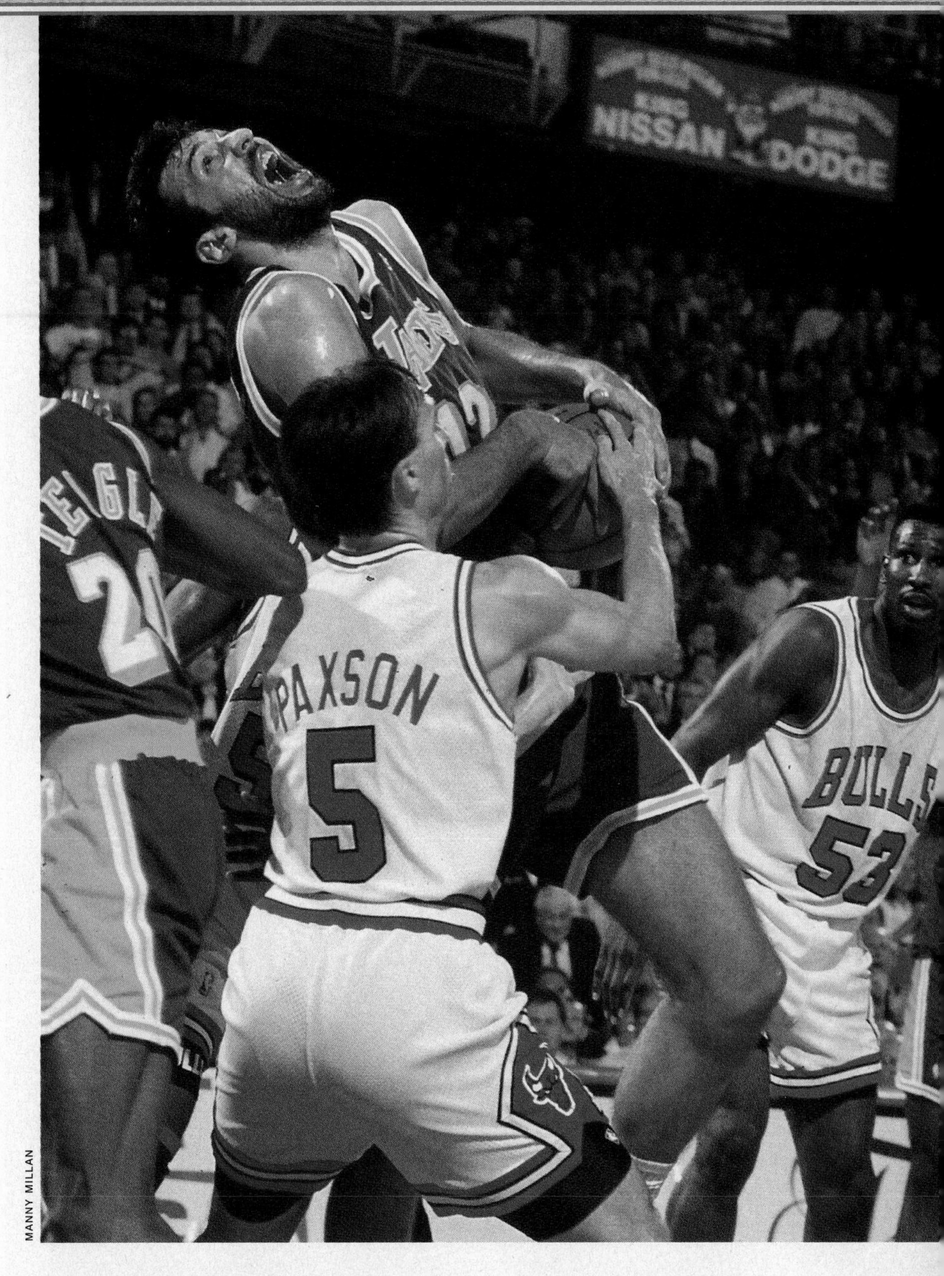

MANNY MILLAN

After losing to L.A. in Game 1 of the Finals, Grant (center, shooting) and Paxson helped to rally the Jordanaires to four consecutive victories.

JOHN W. MCDONOUGH

The Bulls' opponent in the Finals was something of a surprise, though hardly a mystery. The Los Angeles Lakers, considered a bit too creaky to be playing for a ring, had surprised everybody by disposing of the Trail Blazers in the Western Conference finals in six games. These Lakers were no longer the runnin', gunnin', fast-breakin' Lakers of the mid-'80s. They were slower now and featured a halfcourt game built around the incomparable leadership and playmaking of Magic Johnson and the post-up abilities of forwards James Worthy and Sam Perkins.

As much as anything, though, the 1991 championship series was a play within a play, a minibattle between Magic and Michael, the two brightest stars and biggest names in the NBA. No professional sports league is as dependent on the cult of personality as the NBA, and now its two brightest personalities were going at each other, dribble for dribble, smile for smile, endorsement dollar for endorsement dollar. "You can't overhype Magic Johnson versus Michael Jordan," said Laker backup center Mychal Thompson.

From a basketball standpoint Magic, who was nearing his 32nd birthday, could not match the skills of the 28-year-old Jordan, who was still an ascending star. But Magic's game had never been about skills, though he had them aplenty. It was widely recognized that no player of his generation could get the most out of his teammates, squeeze the absolute maximum out of a team, the way Magic could. And those were precisely the qualities that some saw lacking in Jordan's game.

Michael and Magic had been fairly close off the court since the 1987–88 season when Magic, the veteran, took it upon himself to get to know Jordan and to build a bond between them. They had gotten off to a rocky start during the 1984–85 season when Jor-

ANDREW D. BERNSTEIN/NBA PHOTOS

Having given his blood and sweat to the Bulls' cause, Jordan cried tears of joy after winning his first title.

dan, then a rookie, was frozen out at the All-Star Game by some of his Eastern Conference teammates. It was widely believed that Jordan's nemesis from the Pistons, Isiah Thomas, organized the boycott, but Jordan always felt that Magic, Isiah's best buddy, had something to do with it, too. Magic was always vague on the subject, but, whatever his involvement had been, he certainly did not want any differences between them to continue. Magic is nothing if not shrewd, and he accurately perceived that a long-running feud with the NBA's brightest individual star would be counterproductive, both for himself and the league.

Neither star was the most important player in Game 1 at Chicago Stadium, however. That honor belonged to Magic's long-armed teammate Perkins, who calmly hit a three-point jumper (off an assist from Magic) with 14 seconds left to help the Lakers to a 93–91 victory. To most everyone's surprise, the Lakers went up 1–0.

The Bulls had played, in general, like the Bulls of old: too much Jordan, too little of everyone else. Cartwright, Grant and Paxson, for example, had only six points apiece. Would the team revert to previous form, even though the Lakers seemed less formidable than the Pistons?

No. In Game 2, Jordan was almost otherworldly, hitting 15 of 18 shots from the floor in a 107–86 rout and putting a move on the Laker defense that remains a staple of any Jordan highlight reel. Early in the fourth period he drove the lane and raised the ball as if to dunk with his right hand, but on seeing Perkins slide over to stop him, he shifted the ball to his left hand for an underhanded scoop shot.

Just as satisfying for Jackson and the other Bulls, however, was the performance by Paxson, who made all eight of his shots from the floor. At times, even during the Finals, Jordan had subtly rebelled against the limitations of the triple-post offense, and Jackson had to remind him that Paxson was open time after time.

In Game 3, with Jordan again spreading the wealth, it was much the same thing. During a third-period run that erased a 67–54 Laker lead, eight different Chicago players scored, and Jordan had only two free throws. Of course, it was Jordan who sent the game into overtime on a 14-foot jumper with 3.4 seconds left, and he who dominated the extra five-minute period in a 104–96 win.

That victory seemed to take the air out of L.A., which was struggling to figure out Bach's double-teaming rotations. The Bulls coasted to a 97–82 win in Game 4, and, on a glorious Wednesday evening at the Forum, they won the franchise's first title with a 108–101 Game 5 victory that was easier than the final score indicated.

When it was over, the reactions of Jordan and Krause, long-time adversaries, were identical. Both were overcome with joy, the latter because he had taken so much criticism for not getting Jordan enough help, the former because the victory assured that his place in the Hall of Fame would not include the odious asterisk—did not win a championship. ■

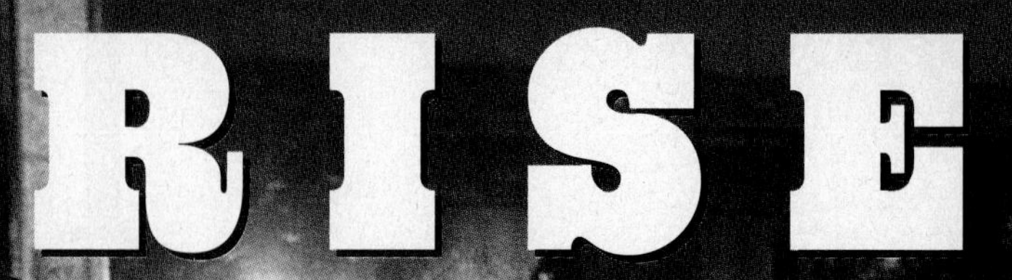

Pippen didn't lie low during this year's playoffs.

AND SHINE

That's precisely what Scottie Pippen has done in soaring above the criticism that he isn't tough enough for the NBA

BILL SMITH

BY LEIGH MONTVILLE

He remembers that he felt the same way after both of the bad games. They both seemed to end in a surreal blur. It seemed almost as if he were a character in a bad movie he also was watching. Stop. Wait a minute. This can't be happening. Let's start over again. Everyone go to his mark. Ready? Let's take it from the top. Let's get it right this time.

There was the external Scottie Pippen whom everyone could see, including himself, the Scottie Pippen who had left the basketball floor at the worst possible time, the Scottie Pippen whose absence meant the downfall of his team in the biggest games it had ever played. Wasn't this guy a true sad sack? A flat-out, high-profile loser? There was also the internal Scottie Pippen, whom nobody could see except himself. The internal Scottie Pippen was furious.

"At the end of both games I wanted to say, Can we play this game all over again?" he says now. "I wanted to say, Can we stop everything and start again? Right now?"

The first year was 1989. The Bulls were on the rise. Pippen was in his second season, a young guy from the tiny University of Central Arkansas who had arrived to play Tonto to Michael Jordan's death-defying Lone Ranger, complete with the *William Tell Overture* in the background. The hurdle was the Detroit Pistons in the Eastern Conference finals. The Bulls were trailing, three games to two in the best-of-seven series, and in the first minute of the sixth—and ultimately deciding—game, Pippen was knocked out by an elbow from Piston elbow specialist Bill Laimbeer. He never returned.

Never returned? In the biggest game of his life? The Bulls lost.

The next year, 1990, was a repeat. Pistons again. Eastern finals. Seventh game this time. Pippen came down with a migraine headache. The pictures that appeared the next morning showed him sitting on the bench with a comic-strip ice bag perched on his head, a long towel and a long face completing the image. The captions indicated

Pippen travels in style, both by land and by sea.

Scottie made a move; he came in from the right and banked the ball off the backboard with his left hand. That's a pretty difficult move, and he did it easy. And when he'd go up the middle? Dunk City."

The NBA tryout camps were Pippen's coming-out party. No one really knew who he was. Because of his size and stats he was projected as a fourth-round draft choice. No one really had seen him. The camps were held in Portsmouth, Va., Honolulu and Chicago. By the time they were finished, the projections on Pippen had changed dramatically. Krause was maneuvering feverishly to secure the fifth pick in the entire draft to get Pippen.

"I'd never seen him until Portsmouth," Krause says. "They come out for warm-ups. They haven't even shot the ball. Here's this guy, he's got the longest arms I've ever seen. I've always been very big on long arms and big hands. I say, 'Holy ——, there's something special.' I look around. Everybody's murmuring."

Krause says he was on the phone with the Seattle SuperSonics for two days working a deal. The Bulls had the eighth pick. The Sonics had the fifth. Krause was terrified that the Sacramento Kings, selecting sixth, would take Pippen. The deal was clinched at four o'clock in the morning on the day of the draft. The Sonics would switch choices with the Bulls in the first round for assorted considerations if—and only if—someone they wanted was not available in the fifth spot. They would not say who it was they wanted. Krause would not say whom he wanted.

During the draft the lines were open between Chicago and Seattle. The deal was not completed until the Los Angeles Clippers chose Reggie Williams fourth. Williams was the player the Sonics wanted. So Seattle selected Pippen fifth, then dealt him later in the day to Chicago for Olden Polynice, the player the Sonics had ordered the Bulls to take eighth.

The freshman manager of a small-college team became, at the end of four years, the player picked to take the pressure off the beleaguered Jordan. Remember the talk of Jordan and the backup Jordanaires? Pippen had been picked to be second soloist in the group.

"It's amazing how far he has come," his agent, Jimmy Sexton, says. "You think about where he started, this quiet kid from Arkansas who nobody had ever

BILL SMITH(2)

Scottie's mom, Ethel, agrees: Good things come in threes.

JOEY IVANSCO

heard of. I was down at Oklahoma State, and one of the assistant coaches there, a guy named Russ Pennell, came up to me and said that he went to college with Scottie. He was a senior when Scottie was a freshman. Russ said he was watching a game on television and Scottie was just doing everything and all Russ could think was, Scottie Pippen—I remember when he was handing me my gym shorts and socks."

"People always ask what would have happened if he had gone to another team, a team that didn't have Michael," Krause says. "They say, 'Well, Scottie would have been a star right away instead of having to wait.' I don't think so. I think coming here made it easier for him. If he had gone to another team—a kid from Arkansas, picked from an NAIA school, picked fifth in the draft—the pressure would have been unbelievable. He would have been asked to produce right away. Here there was no pressure in the beginning. Michael took all the pressure. Scottie had time to grow. He had problems for a while, didn't know how hard practices would be, didn't know a lot of things. He learned from Michael. It was like going to Cincinnati and learning from Oscar Robertson. What could be better?

"I think coming here gave him a chance to be a star. And he took it."

The Pippen of these playoffs seemed to be at ease with himself.

The "soft" business is finished now. Isn't it? The supposed oleomargarine heart has calcified. Hasn't it? The wish to replay the big game, the biggest game in his life, has been granted to Pippen again and again and yet again, and he has responded on every occasion. Three championship rings are his evidence. Not to mention an Olympic gold medal.

The final testimony in his defense was given this spring on the floor of Madison Square Garden. The New York Knicks and the New York press had brought back all of the old stories. Pippen was the underbelly of the Bulls' operation, the soft spot that could be attacked. The Knicks were the barroom bullies who would make Pippen run for cover. Get the ice bags ready. The Knicks would take care of this girlie-man and move on.

Oh, yes? Who was bringing the ball up the floor against the Knicks' karate defense? Who was sticking the tough jumpers with time running down, while Jordan was double-covered or struggling with his shooting? Who was there at the end of Game 5, the turnaround game at the Garden, swatting away the final two of Charles Smith's four shots from under the basket, any of which would have changed the outcome? This was the place Pippen wasn't supposed to be, in the middle of the elbows and the heat. These were the things he wasn't supposed to do. These were the things he did.

"I love the challenge," he says. "I loved it when the Knicks said they were coming after me. I hoped Phoenix would do the same thing. During the Knick series I felt really healthy for the first time all season. [He had been slowed for much of the year by a sprained left ankle; a cortisone shot he received a month before the playoffs had helped.] When I'm healthy there isn't a challenge in the world I can't meet."

Pippen's statistics went on a straight progression upward, increasing with almost each playoff series, from 15.3 points and 4.0 rebounds in the opening series against the Atlanta Hawks, to 18.3 points and 6.3 rebounds against the Cleveland Cavs, to 22.5 points and 6.7 rebounds against the Knicks, to 21.2 points and 10.9 rebounds against the Suns. His importance in the Chicago operation was never greater. With Jordan nagged by gambling controversies off the court and hounded into some bad shooting nights on it, Pippen was a reliable antidote. Still the second banana to Jordan, he nevertheless moved closer to equal billing. With just about any other team in the NBA, he would be the marquee player.

"The thing about Scottie is that he's

INTERNATIONAL TOP SELLING TRUCK AGAIN.

Ranks number one in sales for the 12th consecutive year.

CHICAGO, IL–Navistar International Transportation Corp., once again, has placed first in U.S. combined medium and heavy duty truck retail sales during 1992, and continues to lead in 1993, according to figures released by the American Automobile Manufacturers Association (AAMA).

"This marks the twelfth consecutive year International trucks have ranked first in combined Class 5, 6, 7, 8 sales," says J.T. O'Dare, Group Vice President, Sales/Distribution for Navistar.

As reported by AAMA, Navistar sold 63,842 units in Classes 5, 6, 7 and 8 during 1992 for a combined 28.6 percent market share, almost 10 full percentage points over its next nearest competitor.

"We are very grateful to our customers for making this achievement possible," O'Dare continued. "By finishing first for twelve years running, Navistar has reached a significant milestone and proven that the International brand is, indeed, America's favorite."

WHEN THE CUSTOMER COMES FIRST, SO DO WE.

It's tough enough to stay on top for a few years. Just ask Chicago's World Champions.

But 12 years running? That has to tell you something about the extra value we build into every medium and heavy duty truck.

Maybe it's because we custom build them to your exact business needs.

Maybe it's because of their unmatched toughness and durability. Or our 900 parts and service locations across North America.

To find out for yourself, visit your International dealer or call 1-800-962-0119, Ext. 928.

You'll soon see that because our customers always come first, so do we.

INTERNATIONAL®

BUILT FOR YOUR BUSINESS.

Pippen's glad he is less hounded than Jordan.

MANNY MILLAN

still just scratching the surface of what he can be," Krause says. "I think he'll be a better defensive player, although he's not bad now. I think he'll be a better shooter, although his shooting certainly has improved. You look at him . . . his tools just stun you. He is just now coming into that age range, the late 20's, early 30's, when players are at the top of their games."

"His role here has grown and grown," says Bull coach Phil Jackson. "Starting out, you could see his possibilities. He could rebound yet still dribble. He could post up, but he also had those slashing moves. You knew he could be a very good player, but you didn't know how good. He played a few times at guard in his first couple of seasons, bringing the ball up against teams with pressing guards, but mostly we used him at small forward.

"As more and more teams pressed, however, we decided we had to become more creative. More and more we had to go to Michael to bring the ball up. We didn't want to do that. We came up with the thought of Scottie as a third ball advancer, of an offense that attacked at multiple points. From that position he started to take control, to make decisions. He became a bit of everything."

Pippen didn't want to be like Mike. He was happy to be himself.

A bit of everything. The comparisons with Jordan are inevitable—the player who has combined the largest bits of everything to become the best player in NBA history—but even they don't seem to matter anymore. The Pippen of these playoffs seemed to be a man at ease with himself. He didn't want to be like Mike or like anyone else. He was happy to be himself. There have been times when he has fought against his situation, felt it was strangling him. No more.

"I wouldn't ever want to be Michael," he says. "To have to stay in the room all day long because so many people are waiting outside? To always have the feeling that someone is standing behind you, listening, just recording everything you say and do? I don't know how he does it. I can go out, I can walk around. People come up to me for autographs and talk, but it's natural. They see Michael and they jump. People act as if they've seen a ghost. I wouldn't want to live like that.

"I honestly don't know whether I could function as a player away from Michael now. What Michael has brought us is the spotlight and the pressure. All of us—Horace Grant, John Paxson, B.J. Armstrong—had to respond to it or else we would have died as a team. Eventually we did respond, and it made us stronger. . . .

"I've come to terms with my role on this team, and that is to do the things I can do. I'll never be the scorer Michael is. I couldn't put up those numbers if I tried. And you know what? I hope he leads the league in scoring for the rest of his career. And when it's over, I'll be able to say, 'I helped him do it. And I played with the greatest player ever.' "

The final laugh again this spring belongs to this tall, 27-year-old man with the elongated face that looks as if it has been taken from a cubist's sketch pad. Soft? He can wink from behind those glasses that he started wearing off the court to ward off eye strain and migraines. He can greet his detractors with civility, knowing they have to erase all the old words they have written about him. He has moved into the movie he once had to watch and has set everything straight. Any questions? All he has to do is show his hands in response.

"Scottie, do you think this was the series when you really proved yourself?" one breathless questioner asked after the playoffs with the Knicks.

"I have two championship rings," Pippen replied. "I don't think I have anything to prove."

Adjust the total. Now he has three. ■

INCREDIBULL!

KILLIAN'S RED CONGRATULATES THE BULLS
ON MAKING IT THREE IN A ROW.

THAT
CHAMPIONSHIP
SEASON
2
BULLS

The 1991–92 season began with some controversial "rules" and ended with the Bulls ruling over the Trail Blazers in six games

BY JACK McCALLUM

JOHN W. McDONOUGH

DAILEY
34
BULLS
23
KNICKS

MANNY MILLAN

Round 2 against the Knicks resembled Round 15 of a prizefight, with a little Paxson and Mark Jackson wrestling (right) on the side.

B efore the Los Angeles Lakers won back-to-back championships in 1986–87 and '87–88 and the Detroit Pistons did the same in 1988–89 and '89–90, there had not been a repeat winner in the NBA for two decades. It had been, in fact, an annual story for journalists who cover the NBA. Why couldn't anyone repeat?

For those close to the league, however, there was an easy answer to that question. It was just too damn difficult to find the same blend of desire, motivation and team chemistry that earned a team its first championship. The Bull team that prepared for the 1991–92 season provided a number of crystal-clear examples of what can happen to sidetrack a defending champ.

Distractions? That didn't quite describe it. After the Bulls won the championship in 1991, Michael Jordan was easily the most famous athlete in the world, and he was spreading himself incredibly thin. One moment he was hosting *Saturday Night Live*, another he was in North Carolina for a ceremony at which a highway was named in his honor, another he was filming a commercial for one of the numerous companies for which he was a spokesman, another moment he and Scottie Pippen were being introduced as charter members of the first U.S. Olympic basketball team to include NBA stars. And all that, of course, had to be fit in between his regular 36- and 54-hole golf orgies.

Even the Olympic announcement was not without its controversies. Though Jordan vehemently denied it, there were reports that he had lobbied to keep his Piston nemesis, Isiah Thomas, off the team, and he took some heat for that. And the inclusion of Pippen, only lately an elite player, on the Dream Team was criticized by some observers, particularly those who remembered him as Mr. Migraine.

LOU CAPOZZOLA/NBA PHOTOS

Then, too, word had begun to spread late in September about an upcoming book that was said to be extremely critical of Jordan. Written by Sam Smith, who had covered the team for the *Chicago Tribune*, it was called *The Jordan Rules* and reportedly contained detailed complaints from other players about preferential treatment given to Jordan. Those complaints seemed to be borne out in early October when Jordan missed what was called a "mandatory" team trip to the White House, where President George Bush congratulated the Bulls for winning the NBA title. Jordan said he was with his family, but anyone who knew Jordan knew that his "family" included a seven-iron.

The troubles continued in training camp. Jordan was late in reporting and testy when he did. The book, released on Nov. 13, was in-

In the Eastern finals, Jordan showed the Cavaliers that if he just hangs around long enough he'll be able to dish off to an open teammate.

deed somewhat anti-Jordan. Some of the Bulls backed off the criticisms they had made of Jordan in the book, but only partially. Relations remained particularly strained between Jordan and Horace Grant, who was considered by most members of the media to be the most forthright member of the Bulls.

In short, no one would've been surprised if the defending champs came out of the gate stumbling.

Instead, they came out smokin'. There were many reasons for this, but they all boiled down to one: The Chicago Bulls of 1991–92 were far and away the best team in basketball. Early in the season the team quickly established a pattern. The Bulls would arrive in a new town, where Jordan and his teammates would be asked about the revelations in *The Jordan Rules*. They would answer that the book was either inaccurate or exaggerated, and then they would go out and tear up the home team. An early-season West Coast road trip set the tone for the whole season. Chicago beat the Golden State Warriors, Seattle SuperSonics, Denver Nuggets, L.A. Clippers, Portland Trail Blazers and Sacramento Kings, all in a row. O.K., Jordan seemed to be saying, you dis me off the court and I'll dis you on the court.

The Bulls spent most of the season chasing the NBA's alltime best record of 69–13, set by the 1971–72 Lakers. They finally fell two games short, at 67–15, but were clearly the class of the league going into the playoffs. Jordan was again the shining star with a league-leading 30.1-point scoring average, but Pippen, who averaged 21.0 points, 7.7 rebounds, 7.0 assists and 1.9 steals a game, was as good a second banana as the game had to offer. Grant also had an outstanding season, and B.J. Armstrong, who had had trouble making his own take-it-to-the-hoop skills fit in the same backcourt with Jordan, had begun to establish himself. Armstrong's 9.9 (oh, let's just call it 10) scoring average for the regular season was a career best. Out in Portland the talented Trail Blazers were putting together an outstanding record of 57–25 in the West, but almost no one noticed them because of the Bulls' supremacy.

Would the playoffs go just as easily for the Bulls?

No. Things never go smoothly when everyone thinks they will.

The Bulls took care of the Miami Heat in three games, which hardly prepared them for the suddenly dangerous New York Knicks, whom they had beaten 14 consecutive times going into the postseason. The Knicks shocked Chicago with a 94–89 victory in Game 1 at Chicago Stadium, then won Game 4 at Madison Square Garden by a score of 93–86 to even the series at 2–2. For the Bulls, the series brought echoes of those terrible days of futility against the Pistons a few years earlier. The Knicks slowed down the tempo, talked trash and banged Jordan and Pippen around in an effort to break their will.

"A forearm, a hip, two hands in the back—they do anything as far as position goes," said Chicago frontcourtman Scott Williams. And Jordan seemed to be nothing more than disgusted. "Their methods are no different from what Detroit's used to be," he said after Game 4. On the sideline even Bull coach Phil Jackson grew frustrated. He was ejected near the end of the third period of Game 4 for repeatedly giving an earful to the referees about the Knicks' physical style.

The Bulls regained the edge with a 96–88 victory in Chicago, but by now an enervating and dangerous seven-game series seemed inevitable. Sure enough, a seemingly tired Jordan missed 16 of 25 shots—22 of them from the perimeter—as the Bulls lost Game 6 at the Garden 100–86. Knick guard Gerald Wilkins, who was probably getting too much credit for "stopping" Jordan, even proclaimed before the decisive seventh game in Chicago that the Knicks had hounded Jordan into becoming a "mistake player."

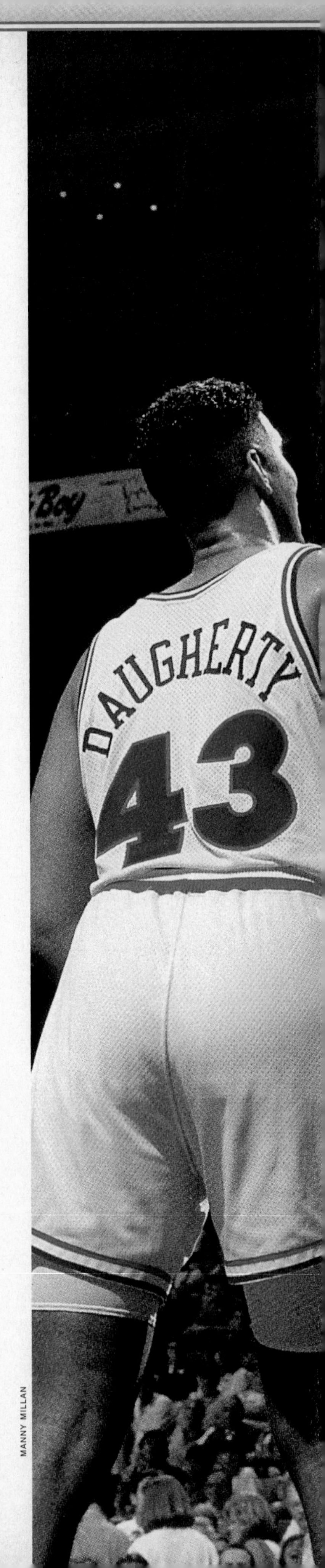

MANNY MILLAN

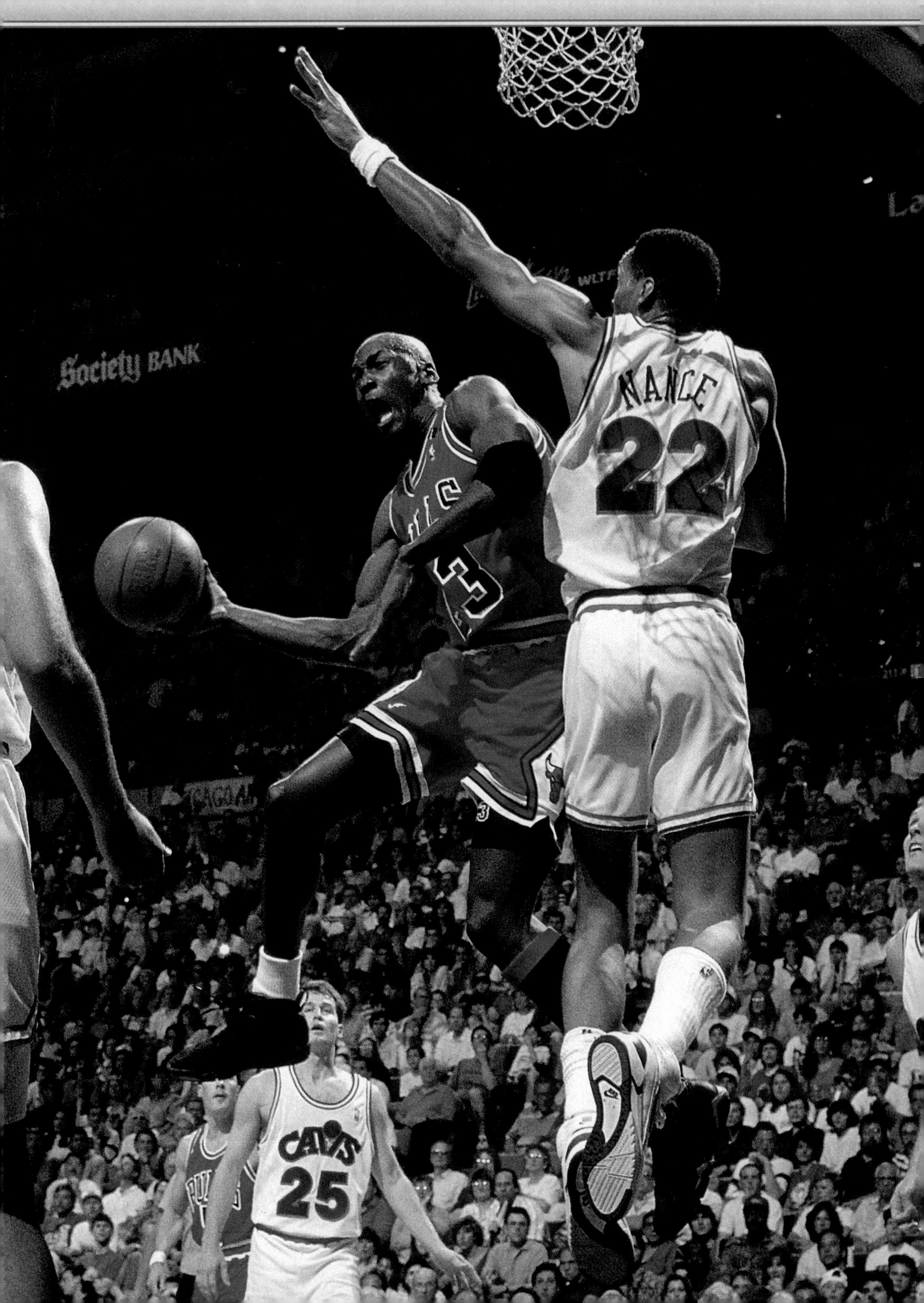
Society BANK
NANCE
22
CAVS
25

JOHN W. MCDONOUGH

Other than on this one loose-ball battle, Jordan got the better of Drexler in every aspect of the game in the Finals.

Gerald, *that* was a mistake. Chicago simply blew out the overmatched Knicks 110–81 in Game 7 as Jordan scored 42 points.

Still, the seven-game series left people divided about what the outcome meant. There were some observers who felt that the Knick series proved the Bulls were vulnerable. But there were just as many others who felt it proved that whenever he had to, Jordan could simply elevate his game and take the Bulls along with him.

The entertaining six-game Eastern Conference finals against the Cavaliers would make no one change his or her opinion. The Bulls won the first game 103–89 and then decided—what the heck?—let's take Game 2 off. They fell behind by a mind-numbing 20–4 at the start (this was in Chicago, don't forget) and lost 107–81. Just as quickly, they turned it around in Cleveland, building a 26–4 lead after eight minutes and winning Game 3 105–96. And then they promptly got blown out again, 99–85 in Game 4.

The series seemed to be a contest between two teams that didn't quite know themselves. The Cavs were obsessed with criticism from the media referring to the team as a bunch of "marshmallows" and "cream puffs." Before Game 3, in fact, Cavalier officials used the scoreboard in Richfield Coliseum to show a scene from the movie *Ghostbusters* in which the giant Stay-Puft Marshmallow Man tramples everything in its path. When the game started, however, the Bulls went out and trampled the marshmallows.

Though they were infinitely more self-confident than the Cavs, the Bulls still couldn't seem to muster the collective killer instinct of true champions, that steely-eyed desire to stomp on everyone and everything that gets in the way. Old problems surfaced too. Both Jordan and Jackson pointed to failures of the bench after the Game 4 loss and Armstrong took exception. "I totally disagree with that," he said. "If Phil and Michael want to point to the bench, then I think it's something that needs to be talked about in-house instead of going to the media." And Pippen, after a desultory second-half performance (three shots, zero points) in Game 4, expressed uncertainty over his role in the offense. "I just didn't get the opportunities," he said. "I guess there were other guys out on the court that were more important."

Still, the Bulls got it back together for Games 5 and 6, winning 112–89 at Chicago and then wrapping up the series with a 99–94 win in Cleveland. Beyond sending the Bulls into their second straight Finals, Game 6 was particularly gratifying for Jackson because Jordan, who did not have a great shooting game for three quarters, was propped up by the solid all-around efforts of everyone else, particularly Pippen, who was still hampered by a badly sprained right ankle suffered in the Knick series. And then, in the fourth period, Jordan took over with 16 points to assure the win.

The individual battle that everyone was waiting for in the Finals matched the league's best shooting guards, Jordan and Portland's Clyde Drexler, who was con-

THE SKY HOOK.

THE NO-LOOK.

THE FINGER ROLL.

THE GIVE AND GO.

THE ALLEY-OOP.

THE SHAKE 'N BAKE.

THE FADE-AWAY.

THE TOMAHAWK.

THE JAM.

THE EDGE. With six rich lubricants, Edge Gel gives you a closer shave with less irritation than foams. Around the NBA, it's the ultimate in-your-face move.

Edge is the Official Shave Gel of the NBA.

MANNY MILLAN

The physical play under the boards seemed to leave both Grant and Buck Williams a little bit goggle-eyed.

sidered Jordan's near-equal on pure athletic ability. In fact, it wasn't close to an even match, and both players knew it. Jordan was far superior to Drexler as a shooter and ball handler and had more grace under pressure—not to mention more off-the-court endorsements and all-around star appeal. The two players mirrored in many ways the Bulls-versus-Blazers series. There was much to like about the Blazers, much championship potential in their roster, but they seemed to have a fundamental weakness when it came to mental toughness.

Game 1 in Chicago Stadium began with a shrug. Not a shrug as in "Who cares?" but a shrug as in "Who knows? Even I can't explain it." That's the look that Jordan flashed at his buddy Magic Johnson, who was sitting courtside as an NBC commentator, after Jordan converted the last of his six three-pointers in the first half. Jordan finished the first 24 minutes with an incredible 35 points to all but finish off the Blazers, who ultimately went down 122–89. Before the series began, when Jordan was asked to compare his game with Drexler's, one of the things he said was "Clyde is a better three-point shooter than I choose to be." So in Game 1 he chose to show up Drexler in that department, too. Drexler seemed to almost physically disappear from the Chicago Stadium floor, taking only 14 shots and making just five of them. Jordan, meanwhile, turned into a passer in the second half and finished with "only" 39 points. That was a calculated move and a wise one, since it enabled the proverbial "supporting cast" to share in the triumph.

Drexler had already fouled out when the Blazers rallied to win Game 2 by 115–104 in OT. Game 2 was as shocking a loss as the Bulls experienced in the postseason. Being unprepared to play, as they were in, say, Game 2 of the Cleveland series was one thing; blowing a nine-point lead in the final 4:09 at home was something else again. Most disturbing was Jordan's lack of composure down the stretch—after being whistled for a foolish reach-in foul, he was hit with a technical after screaming at referee Jess Kersey.

Drexler finally put together a solid performance (32 points, nine rebounds) in Game 3 in Portland, but none of his teammates were there to help him. The Bulls' 94–84 win was a strange one because no one on the team really played well. But perhaps the game's ugliness could be attributed to the swarming Chicago defense, which can throw teams so out-of-kilter that the game suffers along with it.

Did someone say "suffer"? That's what Bull fans were doing after a Game 4 fold-o-rama by Chicago that paralleled the team's collapse down the stretch in Game 2. This time Chicago was up 80–74 with 7:42 left when it suddenly went flat and lost 93–88. Flattest of all was Jordan, who went scoreless over the last 10 minutes and later mentioned (complained, really) that he was tired because Pippen's foul troubles had kept him on the floor for 44 minutes.

BULLISH JOURNALISM

To win an NBA Championship is tremendous. But to win the world title three straight years is an historic sports achievement. And a big reason the Chicago Bulls' phenomenal accomplishment will be so well preserved in history is due to the comprehensive coverage provided by the Chicago Tribune. The tough, in-depth reporting. The challenging commentary. The stop-action photography. It's a journalistic effort worthy of the three-time world champs.

BILL SMITH

Having won a championship the year before, Jordan was better able to kick back and enjoy the second one.

So now the series was tied 2–2 even though the Bulls had dominated all but about 10 minutes of the four games. Couldn't this team that won 67 games during the season do *anything* the easy way in the playoffs?

Game 5 would almost certainly decide the series. Win it, and the Bulls would have two chances to get the title back in Chicago. Lose it, and the Blazers moved into the driver's seat.

One of the game's first plays set the tone for what would follow. With the score tied 2–2, Jordan streaked back on defense, broke up a Blazer fast break, then came back down and drilled a three-pointer. The Blazers could not begin to match the Bulls' ferocity and lost 119–106 to send the series back to Chicago.

Would the Blazers even bother to show up? Whaddya think, Bulls by 20?

No such luck. Continuing its pattern of doing things the hard way, Chicago trailed 79–64 going into the fourth period, which began with four reserves (Armstrong, Williams, Bobby Hansen and Stacey King) on the floor with Pippen. Anyone for a Game 7? But then began the most incredible comeback in Finals history. Hansen, who wouldn't even be with the team the following season, hit a three-pointer and made a key steal. King made three free throws and a jumper. Pippen hit a layup. The Blazers double-dribbled, traveled and threw bad passes. Jordan, after checking back into the game, took over down the stretch with three jumpers, two baseline drives and two clutch free throws.

When the dust cleared and the Blazers were able to shake the cobwebs from their brains, the Bulls had a 97–93 win and were dancing on the scorer's table, fists and champagne bottles held high. The Trail Blazers' Danny Ainge seemed to sum up these Bulls when he said, in a subdued losers' locker room: "I don't think they're a great team. Let's just say they're a very good team with one great player."

Fair enough, Danny.

But how about if they were to win *three* straight titles? ■

First Round NBA Draft Pick

Amway Corporation has just teamed up with the National Basketball Association. Nutrilite® products from Amway are now *The Official Vitamins & Food Supplements of the NBA.* Plus, Amway will be the sponsor of the 1993-94 "Defensive Player of the Year" award. Amway and the NBA have become synonymous with quality performance and successful marketing. It's a winning combination.

Worldwide Sponsor of the NBA

A HEAD FOR

BY JACK McCALLUM

Phil Jackson, a Dead Head and a child of the '60s, is a far better master of the NBA's mind games than anyone expected

THE GAME

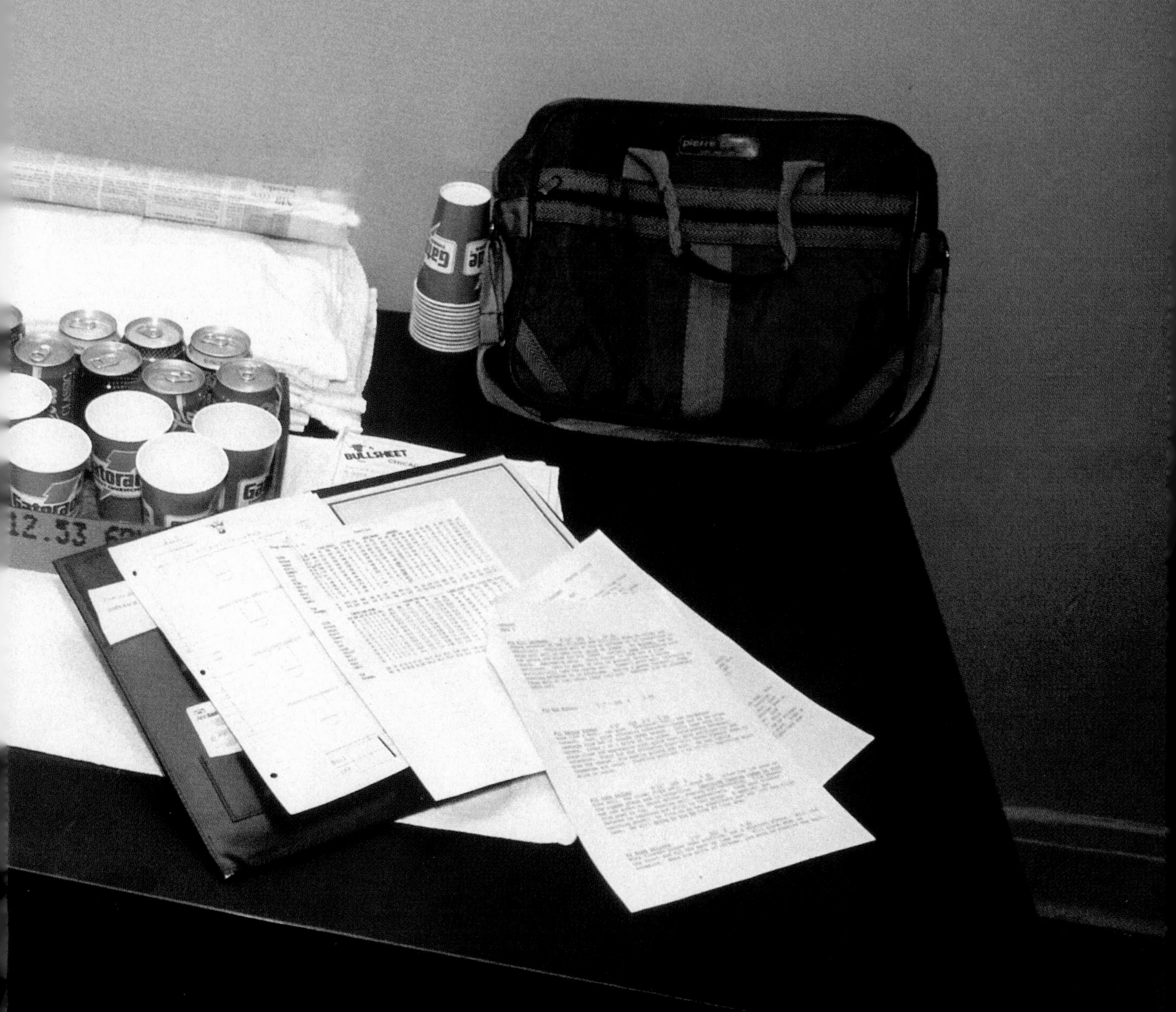

BILL SMITH

Phil Jackson and his wife, June, were biking home from assistant coach Tex Winter's home one evening last month when Phil decided to pick a fight with her.

"It was right after the Knicks eliminated the Hornets [in the Eastern Conference semifinals]," says June, "so Phil had to start getting into his angry power mode. I just happened to be there."

Jackson, the most successful playoff coach in NBA history (his winning percentage is .743), is a man of many modes. One of his strengths is that he is conversant with aspects of human endeavor besides the pick-and-roll, but, make no mistake about it, the tougher the competition, the more competitive Jackson becomes.

Take the Eastern Conference finals against the Knicks, which was in some respects a more arduous battle than the Bulls' six-game title run against the Suns. In his dealings with the media, Jackson relentlessly attacked the Knicks' physical style, offending Knick players, Knick officials, Knick fans and, particularly, Knick coach Pat Riley.

"Pat is going to win at all costs," Jackson said at one point. "He's driven to do that. That's his motivation." On another occasion Jackson proclaimed the Knicks' physical style "fraught with danger" and said that a former player like Riley "should know better" than to play that way. So angered was Riley that before Game 3 at Chicago Stadium, he passed the word through his assistants that he didn't want Jackson to shake his hand before or after the game. True to form, these two proud coaches merely nodded at each other when they passed a few feet apart after the Bulls had clinched the series with a 96–88 victory in Game 6.

Jackson's attack, sometimes subtle, sometimes heavy-handed, was part of a psychological war he had begun last season when he perceived (accurately, as it turned out) that the Bulls' road to an NBA championship would pass through New York. Everything Jackson said or did during the '92–93 regular season and playoffs seemed an attempt to get under Riley's skin and to convince the Bulls that

GEORGE KALINSKY

they were superior to the Knicks. Would one dare call Jackson, this flower child of the '60s, manipulative or devious?

"No," says June, "not in general. But Riley did seem to push that button in him, didn't he?"

Jackson, however, is adept at pushing buttons too. During his tenure with the Bulls his idealism has lessened somewhat; Jackson no longer expects, for example, that most of his players will actually *read* the books that he hands out to them from time to time on road trips. But he still resolutely uses some psychological gimmicks that can safely be called unconventional.

Before Game 7 of last year's second-round series against the Knicks (which the Bulls won 110–81), Jackson recommended that his players go home and rent *Hanto Yo*, a film about a young Native American warrior who must visualize the white buffalo in his attempt to become a man. This is not normal coaching behavior. Horace Grant actually looked for the film and, when he couldn't find it, decided to meditate instead. That was fine with Jackson, a former meditator himself. During this year's series against the Knicks, Jackson spliced into game films a clip from *The Power of One*, a movie set in South Africa in which a black prisoner stands up to his white oppressors. The point was that the time had come for the Bulls to stand up to the Knicks. The Bulls sometimes snicker about Jackson's methods—and Jackson knows it—but they've snickered less and less as his tenure has gone on.

There's a kind of Zen presence about the Bulls—the sometimes superhuman abilities of Michael Jordan, the wizened guidance of assistant coaches Johnny Bach and Tex Winter (a combined 88 years in the business) and, of course, the unpredictable, fuzzy nature of Jackson. Then again, maybe the Bulls just have the best team in the league.

Jackson's greatest gift might be his ability to inspire in his players a sense of freedom, a sense that there's room to experiment and to have fun within the confines of a system. Jackson is a big fan of the Berto Center, the Bulls' luxurious practice facility in suburban Chicago, particularly because it restricts press access and puts a premium on privacy. (Jackson reminds no one of general manager Jerry Krause, but he is only slightly less paranoid about the press than Krause.) Yet on occasion Jackson will bring his golden retriever to the Berto Center and let him ramble around untended. One could not imagine, say, Riley turning his dog loose at a Knick practice session.

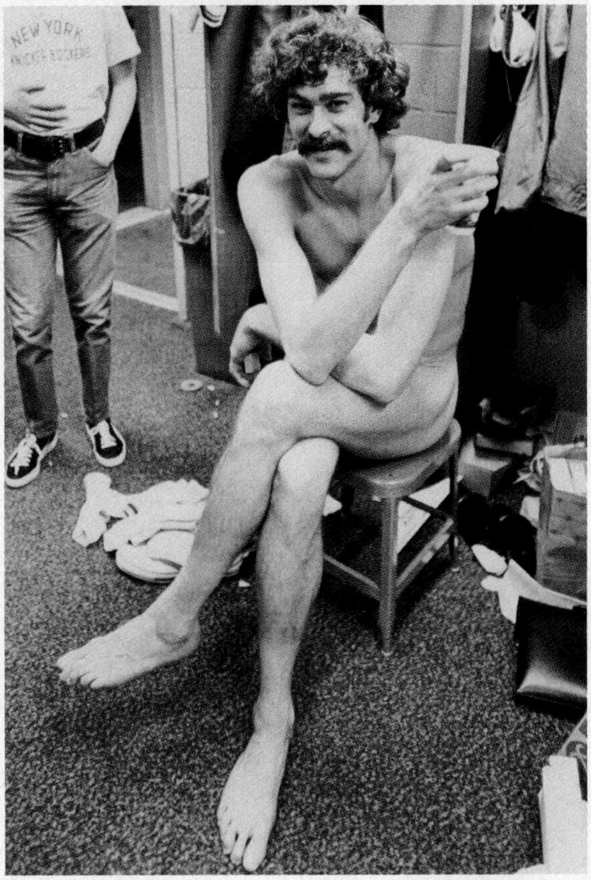

Jackson does get angry on occasion—"Phil has a bark" is the way Bach puts it. And a player certainly doesn't want to be the object of Jackson's scrutiny when the coach folds his long arms and raises his eyebrows with that look of absolute incredulity, the same one-two punch he sometimes gives NBA referees.But to many of the players he remains something of a mystery. "He's the most nonfeedback coach I've ever seen," says former Bull Cliff Levingston. Is that good or bad? "Sometimes good, sometimes bad," says Levingston. "I played for Mike Fratello [on the Hawks, from 1984–85 through 1989–90], and Mike is all over you all the time, maybe a bit too much. But sometimes a player wants to hear from a coach. And you don't get that from Phil."

GEORGE KALINSKY

Jackson never wants to come across as preachy. He hates preachy, and considering his background, that's not surprising. Jackson grew up in the hardscrabble town of Williston, N.Dak., the son of a Pentecostal preacher (Charles) and a soul-saving street-corner evangelist (Elisabeth). He was not allowed to dance, listen to rock 'n' roll music, watch TV, read comic books or play cards. But Jackson does not look back with bitterness on his childhood. It was a strange one, to be sure, but he was not an outcast living in religious exile. In fact, he was a joiner. He was a good student, he sang in church and school choruses, he played three sports at Williston High. That's what brought a young University of North Dakota coach named Bill Fitch to town one day. Some college recruiters were interested in Jackson's high-speed, no-control southpaw delivery from the baseball mound, but Fitch saw a tenacious rebounder and defender in this gawky 6′ 8″ kid. Jackson had a successful, albeit low-profile, college basketball career, and the Knicks liked him well enough to pick him in the second round of the 1967 draft, the 17th player chosen overall.

A turning point in Jackson's life occurred late in his freshman year during a long automobile trip he took with his older brother, Joe, who was then a graduate student at Texas. Joe had become skeptical about his fundamentalist background,

Jackson (18) wasn't a very pretty player (on court or off), but he was a key contributor on the '72–73 Knick title team (left).

GEORGE KALINSKY

Jackson (with June, below) was fond of flannel and iconoclasm in the early '70s.

and his doubts stimulated Phil's own questioning nature. By the time Phil earned a combined degree in psychology, religion and philosophy, he had taken courses from all over the curriculum and had all but rejected his Pentecostal roots. His life had become a quest for knowledge and experimentation, and he remains the only professional head coach in any sport who admits to having used psychedelic drugs.

"I think the myopic way I grew up led to my experimentation," says Jackson, who is now 47. "Everything that happened to me in the 1960s was in tune with my background. The whole psychedelic experience was, as Timothy Leary said, 'a religious experience.' "

There's one thing to remember about Jackson, though. Basketball never took a backseat to what he calls his "peripheral quests." He and his pal Charley Rosen, a longtime CBA coach and something of a basketball philosopher, have a saying: "Basketball's not a metaphor for life. Life's a metaphor for basketball."

Jackson had a basketball mind—if he hadn't, he could not have remained in the NBA for 13 seasons (11 with the Knicks, two with the New Jersey Nets) with his limited scoring (6.7 points per game). Yet no one figured him for the coaching type. Too unconventional, too trippy, maybe even too dangerous. Besides, Jackson had written in his 1975 memoir, *Maverick*, that he couldn't be an NBA coach because he couldn't deal with the egos. Still, when Knick coach Red Holzman sent Jackson to scout games from time to time back in his playing days, Holzman found that Jackson had a gift for "seeing" the game and breaking it down. Late in his career Jackson even served as a player–assistant coach for the Nets under Kevin Loughery.

After his playing days ended in 1980, Jackson ran a health club in Montana for a while, then worked as a Net TV commentator and finally took a job as coach of the Albany Patroons of the CBA in 1983. He interviewed in 1985 for an assistant's job with the Bulls, but Jackson did not feel he was taken seriously by their coach, Stan Albeck. Two years later Krause, Jackson's main advocate on the Bulls, called him and asked him to interview for a position under Doug Collins, and Jackson was hired. By the time Chicago lost to Detroit in the '89 Eastern Conference finals, Bull management had grown unhappy with the emotionally volatile Collins. Jackson took the coach's job, paid one more year of dues, in which he lost to the haughty Pistons, then won three straight titles.

Jackson's greatest triumph may have been in getting Jordan to accept the restrictions of Winter's triple-post offense. "When I got here, there was a feeling of impotence among some players who were eliminated from the process of ball movement," says Jackson. "I came from the Knick system that incorporated all five players. Tex's system made a lot of sense."

That doesn't mean Jordan doesn't dominate the offense, nor does it mean that the coach and the player have it all worked out nice and tidy. Even in the Bulls' most recent championship quest, there were times when the offense suffered from too much Jordan and too little of everyone else. But as Jackson says, "No one said it wouldn't be an ongoing process, and no one said it would be easy." And ultimately it worked, because Jackson and crew now have three rings.

Jackson continues to weave the traditional with the slightly loopy, the same way he mixes his stylish Bigsby & Kruthers suits with psychedelic ties hand-painted by Jerry Garcia, as befits a longtime Grateful Dead fan. Just look at this year's championship series against the Suns. In the final minutes of regulation in Game 3, it was Jackson who told Scottie Pippen to throw the ball off Danny Ainge's back on an inbounds play—a move that led to a Pippen dunk. Any traditional chalkboard coach would have been proud of that play. Yet after the game, here was Jackson cross-referencing the Chicago weather to his team's mental state. "Hopefully the thunderstorm did not only happen outside but internally for the players," he said. Could you imagine Lenny Wilkens saying that?

Another example: Before Game 5 (a game the Bulls lost 108–98, forcing them

HOT DOG! YOU DID IT AGAIN.

Congratulations Michael on your 1993 NBA Championship.

JOHN W. McDONOUGH

Jackson's No. 1 challenge was getting Jordan to go for his offense.

to win the series in Phoenix), Jackson was padding around the Bull locker room about an hour before the game when he suddenly delivered this analysis to several reporters. "Did you know there are three kinds of players in the game?" Jackson asked. " 'Fairies' are anyone under six-four. 'Goons' are players over six-ten. And 'foons' are all those players between six-four and six-ten. I was a foon, for example. Magic Johnson was a fairy who is actually a goon." Then Jackson disappeared into his office, leaving the reporters to ponder what it all meant.

Surprising to some Jackson watchers is that he has grown into the job and shows no sign of giving it up. The time he must spend away from his family, however, gnaws at him every day. The importance to Jackson of his wife and five children was illustrated a couple of months ago when he and three other local celebrities were asked by the Victory Gardens Theater of Chicago to write a 10-minute stage play for charity. Jackson's piece was not about sitting in a coach's office and concocting backdoor plays. It was called *Steel Cut Oats* and took place at a family breakfast table that resembled Jackson's own. "I sat around and thought of the important things in my life," Jackson says, "and that's why I chose this subject." (The reviews of the performance were good.)

Jackson's biggest challenge throughout the postseason, in fact, was trying to attend the four graduation ceremonies that were taking place in his household. He did see June get her master's degree in social work from Illinois at Chicago, and he was home when their oldest daughter, Chelsea, received her high school diploma. But he was absent when the twins, Charley and Ben, graduated from eighth grade. (Phil and June have another daughter, Brooke, who will be a high school junior, and Phil has a daughter, Elizabeth, from his first marriage.)

Jackson zealously protects his private life and often takes his family on the road with him. At this point he evidently feels he can burn the candle at both ends and not slight his team, his loved ones or, for that matter, his innate curiosity.

"Coaching in the NBA means a life of infinite challenges, infinite adjustments," says Jackson, "That's stimulating. That keeps me going."

Assistant coach Bach agrees: "Phil seems to like the work more than ever, to relish the challenge."

The final word belongs to June. "His mentor was Red Holzman, who coached for a very long time," she says. "And two of the men on his staff right now, Johnny and Tex, are coaches who have been in the business for a long time. I think Phil is very comfortable with who he is and what he's doing. I see no end to this." ■

Your tomorrows depend on the future of your long-term investments. That's why so many investors have trusted their tomorrows to Kemper Mutual Funds. They can count on Kemper diligence and discipline to help provide consistent long-term performance. And that's what you need to start building the tomorrows you dream of today.

Call your financial representative for information including a prospectus about Kemper Mutual Funds, or call Kemper at 1-800-KFS-8600 ext.65.

We're Building Tomorrows Today℠

Before you invest in a fund, carefully read the brochure and prospectus containing more complete information, including management fees and expenses. Fund performance cannot be guaranteed and will fluctuate. ©1993 Kemper Financial Services, Inc. 215700

THREE CHEERS!

Before June 20 only the Minneapolis Lakers and the Boston Celtics knew the joy of three straight titles

BY WILLIAM F. REED

Somewhere in his collection of souvenirs Vern Mikkelsen has an ashtray that he lifted from the Copacabana nightclub in Manhattan the night of April 10, 1953, just after his Minneapolis Lakers had defeated the New York Knicks four games to one to win their second NBA championship in a row. "My kids always thought that ashtray was better than a trophy," says Mikkelsen, now 64 and retired from his Minneapolis insurance business. As Mikkelsen and his teammates toasted one another that night at the Copa, they couldn't have known that they were destined to occupy a special place in basketball history. A year later

In '64 Boston was as thrilled with its sixth title in a row as the Lakers were with their second, in '53.

they would become the first team to win three consecutive NBA crowns.

Until June 20 the Lakers were still one of only two teams to accomplish the feat. The other, of course, is the Boston Celtics, who three-peated in 1961 en route to eight straight crowns—a mark that's as safe as any in the NBA record book. Or as Bob Cousy, a member of five of those eight teams, puts it, "That's one record the Celtics will have until they're able to recreate the DNA and have dinosaurs running around the earth again."

The first championship in Boston's remarkable string came in 1959 against Minneapolis in Mikkelsen's final season with the Lakers. A forward-center on that team, Mikkelsen was the only holdover from the Lakers of the championship years and, at age 31, was no match for Bill Russell, Boston's young pivotman who was on his way to becoming the game's premier shot-blocker, rebounder and psyche artist. After Russell had swatted away several of his shots, Mikkelsen figured the only way to score against him was "to get as deep as possible under the basket and use brute strength to take it up against him." It was no help. The Celtics swept the series, and Mikkelsen understood that a new era in pro basketball had dawned.

As the years passed, Mikkelsen grew increasingly proud that only two teams had won three titles in a row. He wasn't at all unhappy when his old franchise, which had moved to Los Angeles in 1960, failed to three-peat in 1989. Nor was he displeased when the team that stopped those Lakers—the Detroit Pistons—had its

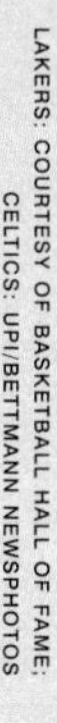
LAKERS: COURTESY OF BASKETBALL HALL OF FAME; CELTICS: UPI/BETTMANN NEWSPHOTOS

Mikkelsen knew a new era had dawned.

three-peat hopes dashed by the Chicago Bulls in 1991. "There's an exclusivity about this," says Mikkelsen, who admits that he was pulling for the Phoenix Suns to upset the Bulls this season. "There aren't too many records left from those days."

Yeah, and the old Copacabana is gone too.

The NBA was formed in 1946, and the Lakers were the new league's first dominant team, thanks mainly to George Mikan, the bespectacled 6′ 10″ former All-America from DePaul. Although he excelled in every phase of the game, Mikan was all but unstoppable when he got the ball near the basket. His prowess underneath led the league to widen the lane from six feet to 12 before the 1951–52 season. Unhampered by the rule change, Big George then led the Lakers to their three consecutive titles. He retired after the last one in 1954 at age 29.

Those Laker teams were the prototypes for today's teams. A center in college, the 6′ 7″, 230-pound Mikkelsen joined Minneapolis in 1949, figuring he would back up Mikan. However, coach John Kundla moved Mikkelsen to forward. "I was a power forward before they had a name for it," says Mikkelsen.

The Lakers also had a brilliant small forward in 6′ 5″ Jim Pollard, an excellent scorer who could rebound and put the ball on the floor. The point guard was the feisty Slater Martin, and the shooting-guard spot was manned at one time or another by Bob Harrison, Pep Saul or Whitey Skoog. In Kundla the Lakers had a coach who was ahead of his time—he understood that psychology was as important as drawing up plays.

"It's very difficult to get together a nucleus of people who know each other and want to achieve," Mikkelsen says. "And it's not easy to get everyone to play his role when you have a superstar. That's where the coach really has to focus on his players and learn how to keep them happy. A good basketball coach could teach a psychologist some things."

ASSOCIATED PRESS

Mikan was all but unstoppable near the basket.

The Lakers, who beat the Knicks in both the 1952 and '53 Finals, got their three-peat against the Syracuse Nationals, whom they defeated in seven games. Mikkelsen believes that if Mikan had played another year, the Lakers would have won four in a row. By then, however, Mikan had grown weary of the punishment he was taking night after night. He had broken at least 10 bones during his career and was scheduled to have his left kneecap removed. Moreover, his skills were eroding. In the three championship seasons, his scoring average went from 23.8 points to 20.6 to 18.1. "He was a marked man no matter where he went," Mikkelsen says. "Everybody knew he was our man."

After a year and a half in the Laker front office, Mikan attempted a comeback at the end of the 1955–56 season, averaging a respectable 10.5 points and 8.3 rebounds in 37 games for a Minneapolis team that finished under .500 for the first time in Laker history. Those who remembered Mikan at his peak found it hard to watch him perform as just another plodder. After that season he hung up his famed number 99 jersey for good. At about the same time, Boston was welcoming a new center who would have an even greater impact on the game.

In March 1961, with the Celtics closing in on their third consecutive championship and their fourth in five seasons with Russell at center, Boston coach Red Auerbach said some things to *The Sporting News* that are rather amazing by today's close-to-the-vest standards. Puffing on his trademark cigar as he sat in his office, Auerbach didn't mince words when asked if his team was as good as the Lakers of Mikan, Mikkelsen and Pollard. "By all means," Auerbach said. "Now don't take me wrong. I have the utmost respect for those Lakers. Johnny Kundla had a great club, and he did a beautiful coaching job. But Boston would have licked those Lakers. For one thing, we have more depth than they had. We have better shooters. Besides, because of the running game we play, they wouldn't be in a position to wait for George."

Indeed, while the Lakers were a team that wouldn't take a shot or begin a play until Mikan had stationed himself close to the basket, the Celtics employed a withering fast-break attack that was usually triggered by Russell's blocks, rebounds and outlet passes. When Russell joined the

"Boston would have licked those Lakers."

Heinsohn and the Celtics flew past the Hawks in '61.

Celtics, before the start of the '56–57 season, black players were a distinct minority in the league. Of the top 20 NBA scorers the previous season, Maurice Stokes of the Rochester Royals was the only black. Russell was to become the game's first black superstar. Or, as TIME wrote in 1960, "The man who turned the Celtics into champions is the lean, agile Negro at center."

To complement Russell, Boston had board-crashing forwards Tom Heinsohn and Jim Loscutoff, and sweet-shooting guards Cousy, Bill Sharman and Sam Jones. The Celtics' other weapon was depth. "When we played them in 1959, we were pretty even five-on-five," says Mikkelsen. "But then, just when we were getting dog-tired, I'd look up, and here would be Frank Ramsey coming off the bench, fresh as a daisy."

With Russell the rookie averaging a league-leading 19.6 rebounds per game, the Celtics won their first championship, beating the St. Louis Hawks, led by Bob Pettit and Cliff Hagan, in seven games in the Finals. The next season the championship series was a rematch, but without Russell, who had injured his ankle in Game 3, and the Hawks prevailed in six. Then came the 1958–59 season, the beginning of the eight-year streak in which the Celtics' final-round victims were the Lakers (five times), the Hawks (twice) and the San Francisco Warriors (once).

Those Celtic teams were similar to the Lakers of their day in that they had little turnover in personnel. Besides Russell, seven players were members of at least five of the eight championship teams. They had a sense of community, and of pride, that set them apart. They also had a pair of extraordinary leaders in Russell, the shot-block artist, and Auerbach, the motivational genius who never let his players take winning for granted.

"Red, he'd foam at the mouth even when he was playing racquetball," says K.C. Jones, who played on each of the eight straight championship teams. "With him and Russell you had that disdain for losing starting at the top and coming right down through everyone."

The Celtics' run was ended in 1967 by Wilt Chamberlain's Philadelphia 76ers. At 7′ 1″ and 280 pounds, Wilt was the most imposing physical specimen the game had ever seen. Yet his team seldom came out ahead against Russell's Celtics—a touchy subject with Chamberlain. So it was sweet revenge for Wilt when he led the 76ers to a 4–1 rout of Boston in the Eastern Division finals. Philadelphia then beat San Francisco to give the NBA a new champion for the first time since 1958.

With Russell serving as player-coach,

It took drive, perseverance and teamwork to make it to the top.

But enough about us...

Chrysler Concorde

The Automobile of the Year* proudly sponsors and salutes the NBA team of the year. Way to go, Chicago. We know what it took.

Your Local Chrysler Plymouth Dealers

*AUTOMOBILE MAGAZINE

"You had that disdain for losing."

the Celtics rebounded to win back-to-back titles in 1968 and '69, giving them 11 in Russell's 13 years with the team. However, their hopes for another three-peat were dashed when Russell announced his retirement in July 1969. Without Russell, Boston was no more successful than the Lakers had been without Mikan. In 1969–70 the Celtics finished with a losing record and didn't even make the playoffs.

From 1969 until 1988 the parity in the league was such that no team won even two titles in a row. In the early 1970s the talent pool was diluted by the upstart ABA, which agreed to a merger with the NBA after the '76 season. Then, in the '80s, those old powers, the Celtics and the Lakers, once again established themselves as the class of the league, but the two were so evenly matched that neither could win consecutive titles until the Lakers slipped past the up-and-coming Pistons for the '88 championship.

Alas, the Lakers' hopes for a three-peat were dashed by the Pistons, four games to none, in the 1989 Finals. The reasons for the loss were as obvious as the mousse in L.A. coach Pat Riley's hair: hamstring injuries to starting guards Magic Johnson and Byron Scott, and the ineffectiveness of center Kareem Abdul-Jabbar, who was playing in the final series of his 20-season pro career.

The Pistons won again in 1990, beating the Portland Trail Blazers four games to one in the Finals, but they saw their three-peat bid ended by Chicago in a four-game sweep in the 1991 Eastern Conference finals. The Bulls then beat the Lakers in five games in the championship round to begin their run of titles.

Cousy, for one, doesn't like to hear any talk that the Bulls might be in the same league with his Boston teams. "There were eight teams when we started, and during the consecutive run, the league only added one," says Cousy. "The talent was far more concentrated, and because you were seeing the same faces all the time, the intensity was at a higher level. I concede the obvious, that the athlete of today is bigger, better, stronger and everything else, but in terms of that particular achievement, I think it's premature to start making comparisons. Let's wait a few years on that."

Chamberlain's Sixers ended Russell's reign.

Mikkelsen, the old Laker, doesn't begrudge the Bulls their success. He is wistful, however, about the fact that he doesn't have any championship rings. Neither the league nor the team provided them in his era. "It would be nice for the grandkids," says Mikkelsen. "They don't really believe old people like me could ever have played the game."

If the kids have any doubt, all they have to do is look at that ashtray from the Copa. ■

THAT CHAMPIONSHIP SEASON

3

JOHN W. McDONOUGH

BY JACK McCALLUM

The Suns were only the last of many challenges the Bulls met in 1992–93

hen Michael Jordan and Scottie Pippen returned from their Dream Team summer, teammate Horace Grant was not exactly waiting for them on the curb waving an American flag. Grant had long considered himself an unappreciated piece in Chicago's grand jigsaw, and it hadn't been easy for him to watch Jordan and, especially, his erstwhile best buddy Pippen soak up the glory in Barcelona. Grant's frustration bubbled to the surface in training camp, where coach Phil Jackson, in an effort to rest his two Olympians, allowed them to basically come and go as they pleased during the first week. Grant bolted practice one day and, in several candid interviews, vented his frustration over the "preferential treatment" and "double standards" that existed on the Bulls.

So it was on a sour note that the two-time champions began their quest to become the first team in 27 years, and only the third ever, to win three straight NBA championships. Moreover, Grant's dissatisfaction wasn't the only difficulty. Both guard John Paxson, 32, and center Bill Cartwright, 35, had undergone off-season arthroscopic surgery on aging and battered knees. In fact, so many players were riding so many stationary bikes during early October that the Berto Center, the Bulls' practice facility, looked as if it were hosting the U.S. cycling team rather than an NBA training camp.

Also, with Paxson's effectiveness limited, Jackson was again faced with the dilemma of whether to elevate B.J. Armstrong into the starting lineup. The 25-year-old Armstrong was a far better penetrator and a more nimble defensive player than Paxson, but Jordan had consistently stated that he thought Paxson better complemented his own game. Most ominous of all for the Bulls was the presence of two formidable challengers: the cocky and muscular New York Knicks in the East, and the confident and talented Phoenix Suns, reborn under the sign of newly acquired Charles Barkley, in the West. Both teams were poised—many observers said favored—to defeat the three-peat.

Chicago's history of thriving on adversity was well known, and indeed, the red-and-black locomotive kept chuggin' along despite occasional engine problems. Once the season got under way, newspaper reports quickly surfaced that some players were unhappy with Armstrong as a starter. But the Bulls played through it. The off-season acquisition of veteran forward Rodney McCray proved to be a bust, and the bench was even weaker than it had been in the two previous championship seasons. But the Bulls played through it. Pippen wondered out loud if Jordan had taken too many shots (49) to get a spectacular 64 points in a 128–124 overtime loss to the Orlando Magic on Jan. 16 at home. But the Bulls played through it. Grant had some highly negative things to say about Pippen ("Scottie has become arrogant and cocky," for instance) in an *Inside Sports* article that appeared in midseason. But the Bulls played through it. General manager Jerry Krause continued to alienate several players with his avid courtship of Croatian sensation Toni Kukoc. But the Bulls played through it.

Every time someone would speculate that the Bulls' run was going to end in flames, they would string together a few impressive wins just to remind everyone which team had the last two NBA championship banners hanging in its building. Over one stretch, from Jan. 5 to Jan. 22, the Bulls suffered home losses to the Los Angeles Lakers, the Magic and the Charlotte Hornets. Well, they must be dead, it was said. But then they went on the road and beat, consecutively, the Utah Jazz, the Sacramento Kings, the Los Angeles Clippers, the Portland Trail Blazers and the Indiana Pacers. No, they're alive.

Ewing (33) and his mates battered the Bulls, but in the end it was Chicago that advanced to the Finals.

MANNY MILLAN

NEW YORK
33
34
NEW YORK
3

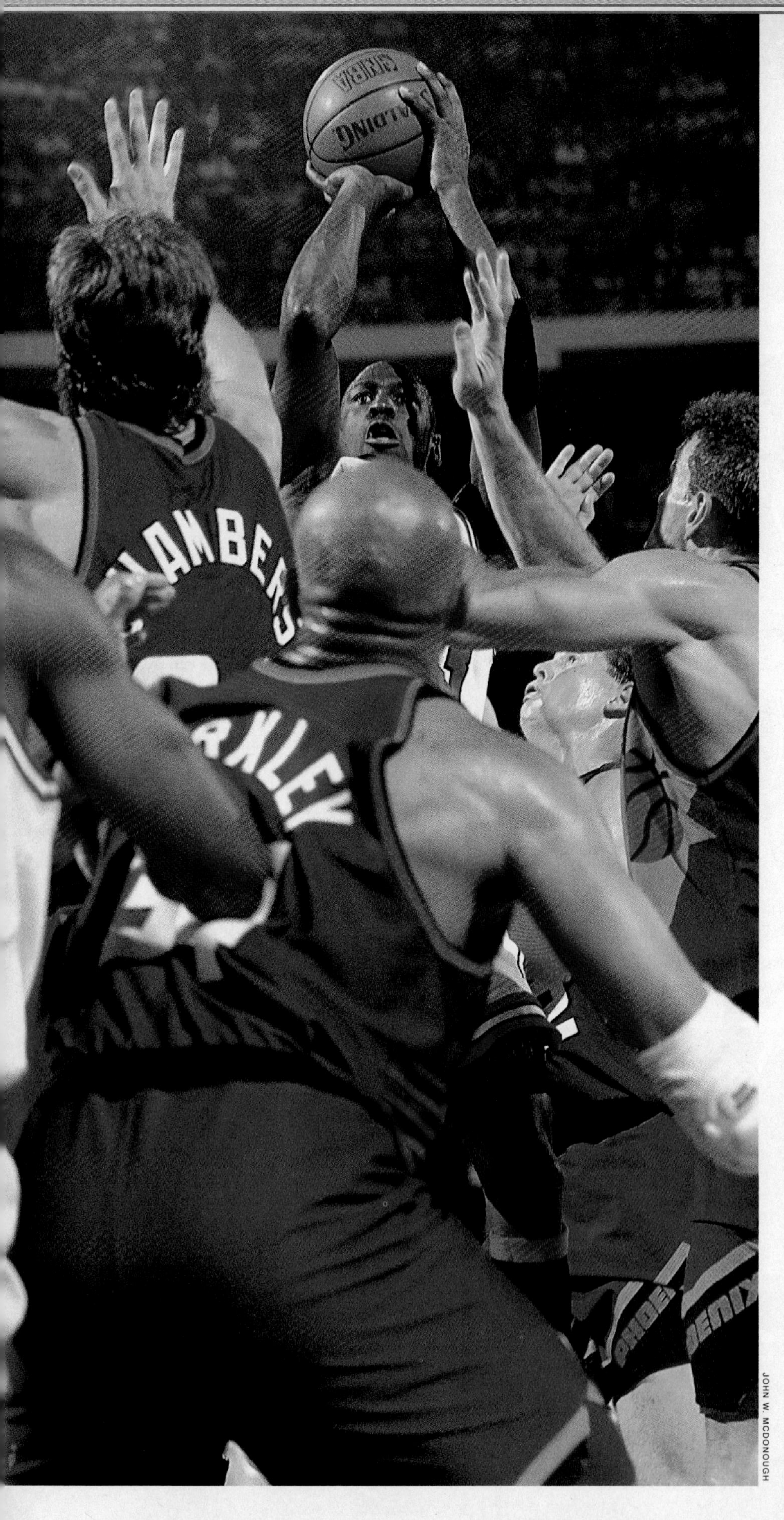

JOHN W. MCDONOUGH

The Phoenix series was an intriguing tale of two well-armed titans: Jordan and Barkley.

"Think of newlyweds," said Jackson one day in Los Angeles, conjuring up metaphors for the season. "The husband comes home right after work every night and falls into the arms of his wife. They can't get enough of each other. After a while, though, it gets a little old, and now the husband starts hitting the bars before he comes home. That's us right now. We're hitting the bars—not literally—and feeling the tension when we get home. All teams that have been through a lot of triumph and adversity together start getting tired of each other. It's natural.

"Then there's the gunslinger thing. You come into town, and everybody wants a piece of you, everybody wants to shoot you down. That's how it is when you're the champion.

"Before the season I anticipated the worst, and so far it hasn't been that. But, no, it hasn't been easy either. No matter how you break it down, success comes down to three things—execution, enthusiasm and healthy bodies. All of them have been more difficult for us this year than they were the last two years. And since we're going for a third championship, something very, very rare in this league, they should be more difficult."

So the Bulls endured, banking on the brilliance of Jordan, the sometime brilliance of Pippen, the hard-nosed consistency of Grant and the calming presence of Jackson. Sure, they lost to teams that they had toyed with the two previous seasons, but never did they drop more than two games in a row, a remarkable achievement in the war of attrition that is an NBA season. Gradually the Bulls and the Knicks drew closer to a showdown on the final day of the regular season that would seemingly decide home court advantage

SUNS
34
SUNS

The versatile Jordan hurt the Suns from the perimeter as well as in the paint.

through the Eastern Conference finals.

Just like that, though, the Bulls lost their edge. Two days before the April 25 showdown with the Knicks, Chicago lost 104–103 to the Hornets in Charlotte, thus surrendering any chance it had of enjoying the home court advantage against the Knicks. Then, in what many observers took to be an omen for the postseason, Pippen had a dreadful two-of-16 shooting game in an 89–84 loss to New York at Madison Square Garden in the regular-season finale. The Knicks finished 60–22, the Bulls 57–25. Chicago looked far too beat to three-peat.

But the Bulls suddenly and unpredictably got their second wind. Perhaps it was just their experience. Perhaps Jackson's long-range plan of saving legs and lungs by cutting back on Chicago's signature 94-foot defensive pressure had worked. Perhaps Jordan was fired up by the expectation that he would probably not win his third straight MVP award (which turned out to be true; both Barkley and Houston Rocket center Hakeem Olajuwon finished ahead of him), despite having led the league in scoring for the seventh consecutive season and in steals. Perhaps all three were factors.

In the first round the Atlanta Hawks fell in three easy pieces, Jordan punctuating Chicago's superiority by returning from a third-quarter ankle injury in Game 3 to score 14 points in the final period, basically on one leg. The Cleveland Cavaliers were next to meet the broom. Jordan made Cav coach Lenny Wilkens pay for not double-teaming him by draining a 17-foot jumper at the buzzer in Game 4 for a 103–101 win in Cleveland. That made Chicago 7–0 in the playoffs.

Next came the beast from the East, the Knicks, who chewed up Jordan and spit him out in a 98–90 Game 1 victory at the Garden. GOAT! screamed one New York tabloid after Jordan made only 10 of 27 shots. He spent so much time issuing mea culpas ("I won't walk away from the blame"; "I told the team I let them down"; "I'm not afraid to say when someone gets the best of me") between Games 1 and 2 that one thought that at any moment he was going to have to take responsibility for the Feb. 26 bombing of the World Trade Center. Jordan was similarly off target—12 of 32 from the floor—in Game 2, which the Knicks won 96–91.

JOHN W. MCDONOUGH

BULLS
porter
10
20

HART SCHAFFNER & MARX
AMERICA'S FIRST NAME IN MEN'S CLOTHING

PURE WOOL

After Majerle got burned in the first two games, KJ took a shot at corraling MJ.

JOHN W. MCDONOUGH

At this point in the series, the Knicks' cocky young shooting guard, John Starks, was clearly outplaying Jordan.

Then, just as rapidly as it had faded, the Bulls' pride resurfaced. Maybe it had nothing to do with Jordan's boycott of the press, but maybe it did. On May 27, *The New York Times* reported that Jordan was spotted at an Atlantic City casino on the night before Game 2. The story so angered Jordan that he clammed up. Perhaps as a show of support for their teammate, but probably as a way of escaping what some players considered to be daily drudgery, most of the Bulls followed suit, and their relations with the media were distinctly icy throughout the series.

Similarly, there was no love lost between the two teams, especially between the two coaches, Jackson and Pat Riley. Once Chicago cut through the Knicks' muscular mystique, however, New York was easy pickings. Perhaps the biggest change in the NBA in recent years has been the ability of an outstanding defensive team to defuse a dominant center with pressure on the perimeter. That's what Chicago did to Patrick Ewing time and time again by hassling New York's guards into turnovers or, at the very least, injudicious use of the shot clock.

Game 3 in Chicago was a 103–83 rout for the Bulls. Jordan poured in 54 points in a 105–95 Game 4 victory that tied the series at two games apiece. Back in New York, Jordan put together a brilliant triple double (29 points, 10 rebounds, 14 assists) as the Bulls won Game 5, 97–94, a victory that all but broke the Knicks' spirit. New York showed up for Game 6 in Chicago, but two huge baskets by Pippen, a jumper from the corner and a three-pointer, were the crucial blows in a 96–88 victory that sent Chicago into its third straight NBA Finals.

The New York series had been, as much as anything, Pippen's coronation as a premier player. Had an MVP for the series been selected, the suddenly consistent Pippen would've probably gotten the nod over Jordan, who alternated streaks of brilliance with long periods of woeful shooting. Still, Pippen knew that the stage in the Finals would belong to Jordan and Barkley, whose spirit and inside scoring had lifted the Suns in three difficult Western Conference playoff series, against the Lakers, the San Antonio Spurs and the Seattle SuperSonics. Pippen would turn out to be right about that.

Several days after the casino flap, a book written by a well-known San Diego businessman named Richard Esquinas was published, alleging that Jordan had run up $1.25 million in gambling debts on the golf course. Would this be the distraction that would finally rip apart the champions? Not a chance. Jordan first answered the charges in an interview with NBC that ran during halftime of Game 1 of the Finals. He admitted to having played high-stakes matches with Esquinas but denied that his debt was anywhere near seven figures. Jordan continued to weave a broken-field route around the inquiries until they had all but run out and there was only basketball to talk about.

And what basketball it was. Jordan scored 31 points in Game 1, a 100–92 Bull victory, and 42 in Game 2, which Chicago won 111–108, thus becoming the first finalist in history to steal the first two games on enemy turf. Barkley was nervous and out of sorts in Game 1 (he converted only nine of 25 shots), and even after he matched Jordan's 42 in Game 2, he did not seem to be enjoying his moment in the sun with the Suns.

Could it be? Was the third title going to be a stroll in the park? Would the Suns even bother to make the trip to Chicago?

Oh, they showed up all right, and, perhaps predictably, the Bulls started to make things tough on themselves. They talked of the distractions they had to deal with back in Chicago—ticket distribution, family members underfoot, parties to plan—and lost a 129–121 triple-overtime classic in Game 3. They talked about the "burdens" and "pressures" of three-peating and squeezed out a 111–105 victory in Game 4 only because Jordan scored 55 points. They watched as the good-natured Suns won the hearts of Chicagoans with their humor, their looseness, their visit to Wrigley Field and Barkley's nightly pub crawl. Phoenix won Game 5 108–98.

The Bulls made jokes about having to drag themselves back to the desert to win the series—Jordan had vowed that he wouldn't accompany his teammates if they let him down in Game 5, and Jackson rued the fact that the trip would force him to give up front-row tickets to a Grateful Dead concert in Chicago—but this was no laughing matter. The idea that the Suns could steal the series, laughable when the Finals began, unfathomable when the

JOHN W. MCDONOUGH

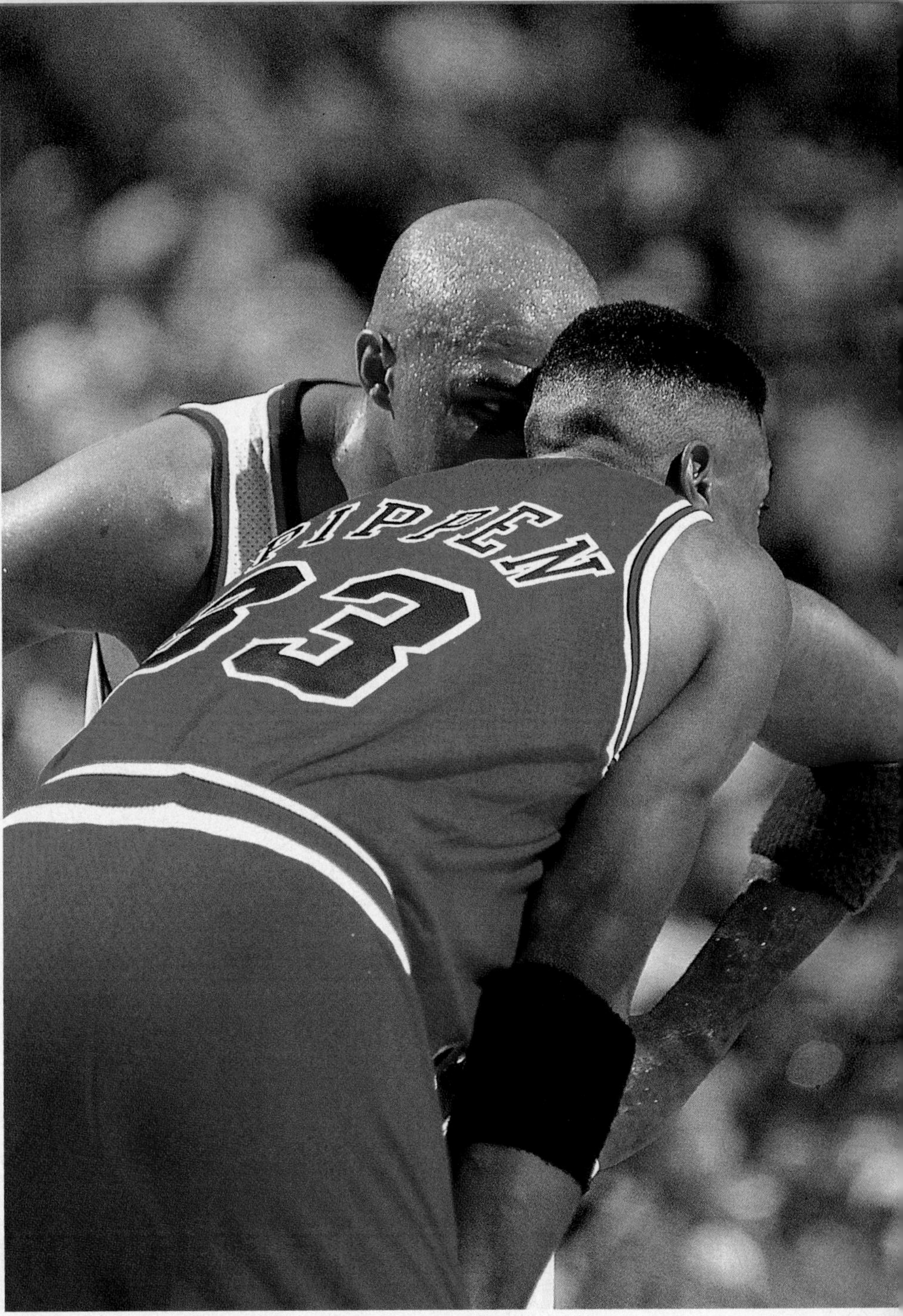

In Game 6, Barkley asked Pippen to stick around a while, but the Bulls refused to linger.

Paxson's title-clinching shot gave new meaning to the phrase 3 for 3.

teams arrived in Chicago only 12 days before, was now no worse than "unlikely."

The Bulls were clearly not clicking on all cylinders in Game 6, and the cold truth was that both Grant and center Bill Cartwright had somehow played themselves out of the offense. Pippen, befitting his unpredictability, was alternately brilliant and terrible. Fortunately for the Bulls, their three-point shooting, normally a Suns' weapon, was clicking. Armstrong, Jordan, Paxson and even little-used reserve Trent Tucker combined for nine treys in the first three periods, which ended with Chicago leading 87–79.

The Bulls, however, seemed fatigued in the fourth period, failing to execute on offense, reaching and holding on defense. On their first 11 possessions of the period, they missed nine shots and committed two turnovers. Meanwhile, five free throws and a Richard Dumas layup allowed Phoenix to draw within a point, 87–86. The Bulls continued to regress, returning to the prechampionship days, a time when everyone stood around and watched Jordan perform, his teammates stopping just short of applauding. In fact, no Bull except Jordan scored for the first 11 minutes and 56.1 seconds of the fourth period, and Jordan couldn't quite keep pace with the Suns. Phoenix led 98–94 when Jordan missed a turnaround jumper with 1:30 left. At that point it looked for all the world as if the Bulls were going to be extended to seven games for the first time in their three-peat drive.

Jordan, though, just couldn't let it happen. "I turned it up a notch," he said later of his defensive rebound and coast-to-coast layup, which brought Chicago to within two, 98–96, with 38.1 seconds remaining. Phoenix forward Dan Majerle, who had been a deadly accurate long-

ANDREW D. BERNSTEIN/NBA PHOTOS

After his game-winning assist, Grant blocked Johnson's shot at glory.

range shooter throughout the series, then air-balled a jumper from the corner, and the Bulls called timeout with 14.1 seconds showing on the clock. All over America, coaches who had been beaten by last-second Jordan heroics got out their mental playbooks and designed ways to stop him.

Jordan threw the inbounds pass to Armstrong, who passed it back to Jordan. Jackson had figured that Jordan would have a better chance of getting to the basket if he gave up the ball and then got it back. So Jordan threw to Pippen in the frontcourt and cut past him. Sun guard Kevin Johnson did an excellent job of smothering Jordan, so Pippen pivoted, looking to take it strong to the rim. However, Phoenix center Mark West stepped in Pippen's path, which left Grant open along the left baseline—but not nearly as open as Paxson, who was lingering behind the three-point line. Grant quickly chucked the ball to Paxson, who launched a shot that temporarily suspended time.

"I knew it was in as soon as Pax shot it," said Jordan. And he was right.

Moments later, after Grant had blocked KJ's final attempt at the buzzer and as the Bulls' celebration began, one could only wonder what at all was left for a man who had won those seven straight scoring titles and been named to the All-Defensive team six straight years. How much better could Michael Jordan get? Which basketball ghosts would he now chase on his way to the Hall of Fame?

There would seem to be only four players with whom to realistically compare Jordan: Magic Johnson and Larry Bird, who were both three-time regular-season MVPs; Bill Russell, the ultimate winner; and Oscar Robertson, whose versatility, leadership and coldhearted competitiveness during 13 seasons make him

JOHN W. MCDONOUGH

NATHANIEL BUTLER/NBA PHOTOS

the closest to Jordan in playing style.

The first two are picked off by the fact that Jordan has guided three otherwise average teams to the title; Magic and Bird made already good teams great.

Comparisons made across the ages are often unfair, but they are most judiciously made by players who have seen both generations. And Jordan gets overwhelming support from two such men, Willis Reed and Bob Cousy, perceptive observers then and now.

"There's no question in my mind that Jordan is the best," says former Knick star Reed, now general manager of the New Jersey Nets. "The guy wins scoring titles, and he's one of the best defensive players of all time. That says it all."

Cousy, a centerpiece of Celtic lore, once selected Bird as his alltime best, but not anymore. "As far as I'm concerned, Michael is Nureyev against a bunch of Hulk Hogans," says Cousy.

Robertson? Well, the Big O's feat of averaging a triple double over the course of a season (30.8 points, 12.5 rebounds and 11.3 assists in 1961–62) will probably never be matched, not even by Jordan. But night in and night out, he did not play Jordan's brand of defense, which on the ball is hard-nosed and off it is a gambling, sneak-into-the-passing-lanes nuisance.

"Oscar was great defensively when he wanted to be," says 67-year-old Bull assistant Johnny Bach. "But Michael is the Tasmanian devil."

When it was all over, after Jordan had been awarded his third straight MVP award for the Finals, after Paxson had been toasted as a clutch player and after all the Bulls had spoken of how tough the three-peat road had been, Krause stood in the visiting locker room, which reeked of the sweet perfume of victory champagne and honest sweat. "You know," said Krause, "I really think the fourth one is going to be a lot easier." ■

Move over, Magic, Larry, Oscar and all the rest—Michael is now the best.

One of the Alltime Greats

When compared with the best pro basketball teams ever, the Bulls measure up

BY JACK McCALLUM

Are the Chicago Bulls a great pro basketball team? Or, as some would have you believe, are they Michael Jordan and a bunch of Dutch milkmaids? I've been going back and forth on this thing since John Paxson sank that 24-foot dagger square into the collective heart of the Phoenix Suns on June 20.

I look at the Bulls' four-headed center—starter Bill Cartwright and reserves Scott Williams, Stacey King and Will Perdue—and compare it with, say, Wilt Chamberlain, the pivotman of the 1971–72 Los Angeles Lakers, and conclude that the Bulls are not a great team.

I see Paxson, nervy shooter that he is, and B.J. Armstrong at the point, and compare them with Bob Cousy from the great Boston Celtic teams of the 1950s and '60s, and conclude that the Bulls are not a great team.

I see the Bulls struggle to score when Jordan isn't clicking, and compare that to watching the Lakers of the 1980s streaking up and down the floor, even with Magic Johnson on the bench, and conclude that the Bulls are not a great team.

There are lots of reasons not to call the Bulls a great team. But I'm going to call them one anyway.

First of all, when most people think of great NBA teams, they think of offense. But that was not the strong suit of the Celtics of the 1950s and '60s; rather, they focused on a defense anchored by Bill Russell, the league's first true shot blocker. The Celtics of that era deserve the tag of "greatest ever" because of their bottom-line achievement: 11 titles between '57 and '69, including eight in a row from '59 to '66. Period.

But almost every other great NBA championship team is defined by its ability to score. The 1966–67 Philadelphia 76ers (68–13 regular-season record) had Chamberlain, Hal Greer, Chet Walker and Billy Cunningham in their starting lineup. The '71–72 Lakers (record 33-game winning streak and best-ever regular-season record, 69–13) were so potent that Jerry West, who had 25.8 points a game while also leading the league in assists, was only second in scoring; Wilt (14.8) was fourth. And when you think of the '85–86 Celtics, you think of the scoring abilities of Larry Bird, Kevin McHale and Robert Parish, perhaps the best front line in history.

The Bulls, Jordan notwithstanding, cannot compete with those star-studded lineups. But they can play defense with any team in history, and that counts for a lot, particularly in an era when defense wins championships. Perhaps the biggest change in the NBA over the last decade has been the ability of a strong defensive team to defuse the opposition's high-scoring low-post player with intense pressure on the perimeter. Teams didn't do that to centers like Wilt or Moses Malone or Kareem Abdul-Jabbar, or even to forwards Bird and McHale. My guess is that the Bulls could've done it to any of those alltimers, not for an entire series, but long enough to win.

How heavily should successive NBA titles be weighed in assessing a team's greatness? In my book, very heavily. Both the '67 champion Sixers and '72 title-winning Lakers returned the following season with their regular rotation intact but couldn't win another crown. Bird, McHale and Parish played together for 12 seasons on the parquet, and though they won three titles, they never won two in a row. The Knick championship teams of '70 and '73 have been canonized and recanonized, yet their titles came three seasons apart.

The Bulls' detractors usually bring up three words: dilution of talent. Yes, there are now 27 teams in the NBA—compared with only nine when the Celtics reigned—and one of them is the Minnesota Timberwolves. But you say dilution of talent, and I say: Late-starting TV games. Early-starting Martin Luther King Day games. Denver altitude. Illegal zones. Four playoff rounds. In seven of the Celtics' eight straight title seasons, they had to play only one best-of-seven series to get to the Finals. What the Bulls have endured is a war of attrition. A team must now win one best-of-five series and three best-of-seven battles to earn a ring; only a great team could do it three times in a row. The Bulls played 304 games over their three championship seasons, including the playoffs. In the first three years of their dynasty, the Celtics played only 260 games.

And there's the added pressure these days of winning under a microscope, which grows more powerful each season. Cousy and Russell could've danced in go-go cages down Causeway Street and it might not have been mentioned in the newspapers or made the nightly news. But the Bulls have lived a daily soap opera that was not only enervating but also potentially lethal to team chemistry. Jordan's life, for example, has become an open book. (In fact, it has become at least three books.) For keeping the saga from poisoning the team, Phil Jackson, step forward, bring your psychology books with you, and take your place as one of the most underrated coaches in history.

If you match the Bulls and other great teams position by position, Chicago simply does not measure up. But that's not what teams are all about. Great teams are better than the sum of their parts, a truism that defines the Chicago Bulls of 1990–91 through 1992–93 and makes them great.

PETER READ MILLER

SHAQUILLE O'NEAL UNPLUGGED.

©1993 S-VC
Gatorade
THIRST QUENCHER
BE LIKE MIKE.™
Gatorade
Gatorade
NBA